# SpringerBriefs in Sociology

SpringerBriefs in Sociology are concise summaries of cutting-edge research and practical applications across the field of sociology. These compact monographs are refereed by and under the editorial supervision of scholars in Sociology or cognate fields. Volumes are 50 to 125 pages (approximately 20,000- 70,000 words), with a clear focus. The series covers a range of content from professional to academic such as snapshots of hot and/or emerging topics, in-depth case studies, and timely reports of state-of-the art analytical techniques. The scope of the series spans the entire field of Sociology, with a view to significantly advance research. The character of the series is international and multi-disciplinary and will include research areas such as: health, medical, intervention studies, cross-cultural studies, race/class/gender, children, youth, education, work and organizational issues, relationships, religion, ageing, violence, inequality, critical theory, culture, political sociology, social psychology, and so on. Volumes in the series may analyze past, present and/or future trends, as well as their determinants and consequences. Both solicited and unsolicited manuscripts are considered for publication in this series. SpringerBriefs in Sociology will be of interest to a wide range of individuals, including sociologists, psychologists, economists, philosophers, health researchers, as well as practitioners across the social sciences. Briefs will be published as part of Springer's eBook collection, with millions of users worldwide. In addition, Briefs will be available for individual print and electronic purchase. Briefs are characterized by fast, global electronic dissemination, standard publishing contracts, easy-to-use manuscript preparation and formatting guidelines, and expedited production schedules. We aim for publication 8-12 weeks after acceptance.

More information about this series at http://www.springer.com/series/10410

Katarzyna Suwada

# Parenting and Work in Poland

A Gender Studies Perspective

Katarzyna Suwada
Institute of Sociology
Nicolaus Copernicus University
Toruń, Poland

ISSN 2212-6368　　　　　　　　　ISSN 2212-6376　(electronic)
SpringerBriefs in Sociology
ISBN 978-3-030-66302-5　　　　　ISBN 978-3-030-66303-2　(eBook)
https://doi.org/10.1007/978-3-030-66303-2

This book is an open access publication.

© The Editor(s) (if applicable) and The Author(s) 2021
**Open Access** This book is licensed under the terms of the Creative Commons Attribution 4.0 International License (http://creativecommons.org/licenses/by/4.0/), which permits use, sharing, adaptation, distribution and reproduction in any medium or format, as long as you give appropriate credit to the original author(s) and the source, provide a link to the Creative Commons license and indicate if changes were made.
The images or other third party material in this book are included in the book's Creative Commons license, unless indicated otherwise in a credit line to the material. If material is not included in the book's Creative Commons license and your intended use is not permitted by statutory regulation or exceeds the permitted use, you will need to obtain permission directly from the copyright holder.
The use of general descriptive names, registered names, trademarks, service marks, etc. in this publication does not imply, even in the absence of a specific statement, that such names are exempt from the relevant protective laws and regulations and therefore free for general use.
The publisher, the authors, and the editors are safe to assume that the advice and information in this book are believed to be true and accurate at the date of publication. Neither the publisher nor the authors or the editors give a warranty, expressed or implied, with respect to the material contained herein or for any errors or omissions that may have been made. The publisher remains neutral with regard to jurisdictional claims in published maps and institutional affiliations.

This Springer imprint is published by the registered company Springer Nature Switzerland AG.
The registered company address is: Gewerbestrasse 11, 6330 Cham, Switzerland

**Funding** *The research was funded by the National Science Centre, Poland, project number 2015/19/D/HS6/02338.*

# Acknowledgments

The process of writing a book is not easy, and even though I am the only author of this book, it does not mean an individualised process. There are many without whose support this book would never have been written. The book is based on research conducted between September 2016 and June 2020 at the Institute of Sociology of the Nicolaus Copernicus University in Toruń (NCU), Poland. The research was titled 'Strategies for Achieving a Work-Life Balance in Polish Society at the beginning of the twenty-first Century. A Sociological Analysis' and was financed by the National Science Centre in Poland under the research scheme Sonata 10 (No. UMO-2015/19/D/HS6/02338). So first of all, I would like to thank all the people at my university who helped me in the realisation of this project. In particular, many thanks go to my colleagues from the Departments of Quality of Life and Applied Sociology Research at NCU—Anna Wójtewicz, Agnieszka Furmańska-Maruszak, Arkadiusz Karwacki, Krzysztof Piątek, Stanisław Burdziej, and Tomasz Leszniewski—with whom I had the opportunity to discuss the structure of this book at the initial stage. With some of them, I had meaningful discussions apart from official meetings, which helped me to develop the theoretical perspective when I was dissatisfied with the work/life balance concept. I am also grateful to Iwona Leśniewicz from the Faculty of Philosophy and Social Sciences at NCU, who dealt with all administrative obligations resulting from the realisation of the research grant. Without her, I would not have made it.

I shared my first ideas and conclusions during multiple conferences I have attended since 2017. I would like to thank lots of people who I met on different conferences—social researchers, sociologists, political scientists, scholars who work in gender studies, and those who specialise in researching economic inequalities. I am especially grateful to the people I talked to after presenting my paper at the XIX ISA World Congress of Sociology in Toronto in 2018, where I talked about the limitations of the work/life balance concept. I received a lot of encouragement and positive feedback, this motivated me to put pen to paper.

This book is based on in-depth interviews with Polish parents. Thus, my greatest thanks go to them. Without their help, and the fact that they agreed to find time for me in their busy schedules, I could not have brought this project to fruition. I am grateful that you shared with me your experiences, thoughts, and reflections about being a parent in Poland.

Finally, I would like to thank my family and friends for supporting me when I was doing fieldwork and preparing this book. The process of writing took place during the lockdown resulting from the COVID-19 pandemic. So special thanks go to Paweł, with whom I was isolated for a few weeks. Thank you for believing in me.

# Contents

1 **Introduction** .................................................. 1
   1.1 Aims of the Book ........................................ 1
   1.2 Methodology of the Project ............................... 3
   1.3 Outline of the Book ..................................... 6
   1.4 My Contribution ......................................... 7
   References ................................................... 8

2 **Parenting, Gender and Work: A Sociological Perspective** ......... 11
   2.1 Introduction ............................................ 11
   2.2 Parenting and Social Changes ............................ 12
   2.3 Parenting as Work from a Sociological Perspective ....... 14
   2.4 Parenting and Doing Gender .............................. 18
   2.5 Parenting and the Welfare State ......................... 20
   2.6 Conclusion .............................................. 26
   References ................................................... 27

3 **Care Work and Parenting** ...................................... 33
   3.1 Culture of Care in Poland ............................... 33
   3.2 "I Can't Imagine My Husband on Parental Leave". Parental Leave as a Mother's Right ....... 35
   3.3 "Nurseries Are So Expensive...". The Care Gap and Organisation of Care After Parental Leave .......... 44
   3.4 "I'm a Bit Down...". Loneliness and Exhaustion in Care Work ... 49
   3.5 Conclusion .............................................. 52
   References ................................................... 53

4 **Paid Work and Parenting** ...................................... 55
   4.1 Is Paid Work a Part of Parenting? ....................... 55
   4.2 "It's Clear That It's Also a Financial Issue...". The Necessity of Paid Work ........................ 59
   4.3 "I Think That a Guy Should Earn to Support His Family". The Different Attitudes to Paid Work of Mothers and Fathers .... 62

|     |     | |
| --- | --- | --- |
| | 4.4 "Time Is the Biggest Problem in My Life." Time Pressure in Parenting | 66 |
| | 4.5 Conclusion | 71 |
| | References | 72 |
| **5** | **Domestic Work and Parenting** | 77 |
| | 5.1 Prevailing Inequalities in the Household | 77 |
| | 5.2 "I Try to Do as Much as I Can". Men and Domestic Chores | 81 |
| | 5.3 "I Just Don't Want to Force Him". Women as Managers of Everyday Life | 84 |
| | 5.4 "I Think It's Fair". The Sense of Fairness and Gender Roles | 86 |
| | 5.5 "We Have a Lady Coming Once a Week". Strategies to Reduce Domestic Duties | 90 |
| | 5.6 Conclusion | 92 |
| | References | 93 |
| **6** | **Conclusions: Parenting in Times of Prevailing Inequalities** | 97 |
| | 6.1 Parenting Work | 97 |
| | 6.2 Opportunity Structures of Polish Parents and Prevailing Inequalities | 99 |
| | 6.3 The Welfare State and Parenting Experiences | 102 |
| | 6.4 What Is Lacking in the Analysis? | 104 |
| | References | 105 |

# List of Figures

| | | |
|---|---|---|
| Graph 3.1 | Provision of childcare. Source ISSP 2012. Prepared by the author | 35 |
| Graph 3.2 | Consider a family with a child under school age. What, in your opinion, is the best way for them to organise their work and family life? Source ISSP 2012. Prepared by the author | 36 |
| Graph 3.3 | Consider a family with a child under school age. What, in your opinion, is the least desirable way for them to organise their work and family life? Source ISSP 2012. Prepared by the author | 37 |
| Graph 4.1 | Attitudes to women's participation in the labour market. Source EVS 2017. Prepared by the author | 58 |
| Graph 5.1 | On average, how many hours a week do you personally spend on household work, not including childcare and leisure time activities? Source ISSP 2012. Prepared by the author | 79 |
| Graph 5.2 | Some people think that sharing household chores is important for a successful marriage or partnership. What do you think? Source EVS 2017. Prepared by the author | 80 |
| Graph 5.3 | Which of the following best applies to the sharing of household work between you and your spouse/partner? Source ISSP 2012. Prepared by the author | 87 |

# List of Tables

| | | |
|---|---|---|
| Table 4.1 | Employment rate of adults by sex and number of children—Poland | 57 |
| Table 5.1 | Who in your household usually performs the following household duties? | 80 |

# Chapter 1
# Introduction

> *For me the concept of 'balance' is somehow strange, because it ... assumes something like segregation or maybe even hierarchy of some elements of me, me as a person. You know? What is more important, what is less important ... So, no – I don't buy it! [C3M4 Paweł]*

**Abstract** The first chapter is of introductory character. I set the aims of my analysis which is based on the in-depth interviews about the reconciliation of parenthood and paid work. The book resolves around the narratives of 53 parents of children aged 0–8 years living in Poland. The interviewed parents differ in terms of social and economic backgrounds, family situation (coupled and single parents, divorced parents, reconstituted families) and place of living (countryside, small, medium and large cities). I describe the research sample and methodological choices I made during my fieldwork. These introductory remarks lead to a summary of the main themes of the book: parenting in the context of the organisation of paid work, care work and domestic work, gender and economic inequalities, as well as the role of the welfare state. This chapter ends by looking ahead through summaries of each of the following five chapters.

**Keywords** Parenthood · Paid work · Care work · Domestic work · Poland · Family policy

## 1.1 Aims of the Book

Recent discussion on parenthood in the social sciences has concentrated on the work/life balance, i.e. how people manage to combine and fulfil the obligations resulting from different roles they play in everyday life. Such an approach focuses on two aspects of life that are crucial for parents in contemporary societies—paid work in the labour market and relations with children that are based on care obligations. The construct of a work/life balance seems to be a handy theoretical tool that helps in the analysis of parenting experiences today. Therefore, when in 2015 I started to consider how to research parenting experiences in contemporary Polish society, I decided to use the conceptual framework of the work/life balance. The main aim of my project was to identify strategies for combining work and family life adopted by Polish parents of children under eight. To do that, I conducted in-depth interviews with 53 parents who had different economic and family situations. Already at the stage of undertaking the fieldwork, it turned out that my aim would be hard to achieve. The experience of parenting described by my interviewees indicated that in many cases it was very difficult to actually set the boundary between paid work and the rest of their lives. In some cases the boundaries between paid work, care work and domestic work were blurred—for example in the situation of parents having their own animal farms or parents with disabled children. Other cases indicated that contrary to the hidden assumption in the construct of a work/life balance, paid work does not hinder parenting, but rather enables it, helping people to fulfil their parental obligations. Finally, many interviewees were not satisfied with their jobs, so for them the problem was not combining paid work with parenting, but rather the unsatisfactory working conditions of the Polish labour market. Consequently, some of the interviewees, those who were more reflexive, critically approached the concept of a work/life balance and did not accept it, as in the case of Paweł, whose words introduce this book.

My aim here is thus to move away from thinking in terms of a work/life balance when it comes to parenthood in contemporary societies. I claim here that this construct is not only inadequate to describe the experiences of various parents, especially those who do not fit the model of dual-earners, such as middle-class couples living in big cities, but also, following Alvin Gouldner's reasoning, is a theoretical concept that is loaded with value judgements that promote a particular *normal/permitted* world (Gouldner 1970). In this world all individuals are expected to work for pay and gain satisfaction from it, yet at the same time they should not spend *too much time* on paid work in order to free up time to spend with their families. As I argue in Chap. 2, the construct of a work/life balance is based on several hidden assumptions that derive from particular views and norms on how society should be organised. Consequently, these assumptions fail to take into account the experiences of people who do not fit this *ideal* model and do not provide a reliable description of social reality. This book is written from a sociological perspective, so its aim is to critically analyse what is happening in family life in the contemporary institutional settings of one European society.

I concentrate here on the experience of parenting in Polish society at the beginning of the twenty-first century. My analysis does not only concentrate on how men and women engage in parenting and fulfil their role of parents, but also shows how individuals' behaviours are grounded in the broader social and institutional context shaped by the welfare state and its various instruments. I claim here that the ways men and women engage in parenting result not only from their personal choices and preferences, but also from *opportunity structures* that are determined by the family policy system, organisation of the labour market, cultural norms about care, and structures of social, in particular gender, inequalities. Thus the aim of this book is to examine how Polish parents deal with various obligations arising from having children. This subject also serves as a pretext to observe contemporary Polish society through a critical lens, one which reveals how various forms of social inequalities in family life are maintained and reproduced by the welfare state. To do so I refer to several theoretical perspectives, in particular the theory of 'agency and structures' as well as the concept of *doing gender*. The theories of agency show how individual choices are grounded in broader structures that limit people's actual behaviours. I am especially interested in how individuals deal with their parental obligations in particular structures that derive from the institutional solutions of the Polish welfare state, as well as how they do so within dominating cultural norms about motherhood and fatherhood, care work, paid work and gender roles. The concept of *doing gender* helps to grasp how various gender inequalities are reproduced and sometimes reconstructed in everyday life. The parenting experiences of men and women significantly differ, and these differences cannot be solely explained by the biological differences between men and women, but rather are grounded in the social structures of a patriarchal society. Last but not least, parenting experiences are not only affected by gender inequalities, but also many other social inequalities that are characteristic of Polish society. Therefore, in my analysis I also look at the parents' economic resources and try to depict how they determine the opportunity structures of different parents. The perspective of economic inequalities, even though quite obvious, is not often adopted in describing the experiences of parenthood in contemporary European societies.

## 1.2 Methodology of the Project

This book is based on a research project entitled 'Strategies for Achieving a Work-Life Balance in Polish Society at the beginning of the 21st Century. A Sociological Analysis' that was funded by the National Science Centre in Poland from 2016 to 2020 (decision number UMO-2015/19/D/HS6/02338). The goal was twofold. One of my aims was to identify how people combine parenthood with paid work to achieve a work/life balance. The second aim concentrated on the organisation of care and domestic work in Polish households. In both of these aims the perspective of inequalities in economic status and gender was very important. To achieve these goals I designed research consisting of three elements that according to a mixed-method approach would describe and analyse a social phenomenon in its complexity to produce more knowledge on the matter (Moran-Ellis et al. 2006). By applying different methods, I attempted to gather different data from various sources that consequently helped to understand the diverse dimensions of parenthood experiences in contemporary Polish society, in particular to grasp the dimensions of inequalities in economic status and gender. Such an approach is characteristic for a triangulation strategy in which using different methods helps to collect data about one social phenomenon 'from multiple perspectives and in different contexts' (Rothbauer 2008, p. 893). Thus my research consists of three parts. Firstly, there is analysis of the Polish family policy system (in Chap. 2). I was particularly interested in how the system had changed in recent decades and how it shaped opportunity structures for parents in the 2010s. I refer here to different theories of the welfare state, in particular to the concept of genderisation proposed by Steven Saxonberg (2013), and try to answer the question of how different instruments of family policy affect prevailing gender inequalities. This analysis was based on government documents containing justifications for the reforms introduced from 2010. Analysis of the Polish family policy system is important to outline the background for describing the experiences of Polish parents.

The second part is based on the quantitative data gathered by Polish and European statistical offices, as well as on data from the European Value Survey (EVS) and the International Social Survey Programme (ISSP) module 'Family and Changing Gender Roles'. Both of these survey programmes are large-scale, longitudinal research which include questions about paid work, care work and domestic work, as well as attitudes to and beliefs about gender roles and family life. My analysis concentrates on 2017 EVS data on Polish society, whereas for the ISSP data is taken from 2012. Additionally, in Chap. 5 on domestic work I refer to survey data from the Public Opinion Research Centre in Poland (CBOS), which conducts regular studies on the division of domestic work in Polish households. The last edition of the study was conducted in 2018. Similarly, as in the case of analysis of the Polish family policy system, survey data serves to provide a background for analysis drawn from in-depth interviews with Polish parents. Additionally, all this data from CBOS/EVS/ISSP complements the qualitative analysis with a quantitative element to create a more robust foundation from which deductions may be formulated to apply more generally to society as a whole.

Finally, the third part of my research project is based on in-depth individual interviews conducted with Polish parents between June and October 2017. In total 53 parents were interviewed.[1] The aim was to examine how Polish parents deal with various obligations arising from parenthood and paid work. These interviews focused on the organisation of care work for small children and how this is reconciled with paid work, therefore the interviews were conducted with parents of children aged 1–8. The preschool years are the most demanding for parents in terms of care work. Small children require lots of attention and cannot be left alone without a caregiver. During this period working parents rely on outside support, in particular from the welfare state and family members. The interviews were based on the semi-structure guides that were divided into three parts. The first part was about the organisation of everyday life, in particular on how care and domestic work were carried out. The second part concerned the situation in the labour market of the interviewed parent, their approach to paid work, as well as relations with employers and co-workers. In the third part, parents were asked how they used different instruments of family policy, in particular how they used parental leave, if they

---

[1] I personally conducted 32 interviews. The rest of the interviews were carried out by other researchers prepared by me, who followed the same interview scripts.

## 1.2 Methodology of the Project

sent their children to nurseries and/or kindergarten, and how they used cash benefits from the 'Family 500+' government programme. The aim was to encourage parents to express reflexive considerations on how they organised everyday life. The qualitative approach brought forward the perspective of an individual who functions in particular social, cultural and institutional contexts. I assumed that the interviewed parents were reflexive agents who could assess their situation and their opportunity structures resulting from external factors. And indeed, regardless of their level of education, parents willingly shared their reflections about institutional settings. The experiences of interviewees show how parents make use of existing possibilities and deal with their restrictions. Additionally, they help to identify how individuals interpret their life situation (Denzin and Lincoln 2005; Heyink and Tymstra 1993).

The collection of interviewees was based on purposive sampling. At the beginning interviews were conducted with parents who responded to my announcement about the project on the internet (mostly from parenting groups on social media), in childcare institutions and on playgrounds. Then I used a snowball sampling method. The sampling purposively included parents in different family situations, as well as in different socio-economic situations, different labour market situations, or living in different places (cities, towns or the countryside). As a result, 53 parents were interviewed (29 mothers and 24 fathers) aged 24–48. Most interviewees worked full-time, only six interviewees were unemployed and six were on extended parental leave. Forty interviews were conducted with coupled parents, but each person from the couple was interviewed separately. Thirteen interviewees were single parents (eight mothers and five fathers). Five parents had at least one child with a severe disability. Thirteen interviewees lived in the countryside or a town, 22 in small cities, and 18 in big cities. Six parents were in a very good financial situation and did not worry about money at all. Ten parents experienced severe difficulties in making ends meet. The remaining interviewees had an average financial situation, they could meet basic needs, although could not always afford one-off expenses, and so needed to carefully calculate their everyday budgets. All coupled parents were in a heterosexual relationship, though two single mothers either at the time of interview or previously had been in a relationship which was not heteronormative—one was in a relationship with a woman, the other in a relationship with a trans man. As this latter group only amounted to two individuals this did not warrant the creation of a separate category in my analysis.

All interviews were recorded and transcribed. All interviewees were guaranteed confidentiality, thus all names and personal details that might identify a person have been changed in the citations used in this book. I also decided not to include the age, level of education or occupation of the interviewees, nor the age of children, this is to make it more difficult to identify people based on the fragments of the interviews. There are several reasons for this. I shall focus on two of them. First, the researched individuals were reassured about confidentiality and that the information shared during the interview would not be shared with other people, in particular their partners. Family life can be an area of great conflict and not all disagreements can be solved by a couple. Couples do not always share similar opinions about gender roles, family models, or how to raise children. During the interviews individuals often complained about their partners. Since this book is available to everyone, I need to ensure that my interviewees cannot be identified by the citations. Secondly, parenthood, gender roles and the organisation of care work are not value-free. The opinions shared by the interviewees were very different—some of them were more conservative, others represented a more equalitarian approach to many issues connected to parenthood. During the analysis it is not always possible to maintain neutrality, especially if the researcher tries to provide a critical analysis of the social phenomenon. Thus I know that not all interviewed parents would be happy with my reasoning and conclusions, especially about gender inequalities. That is why I have attempted to make it difficult for my interviewees to recognise themselves in the citations. I do not want them to feel upset by my interpretations of their words. At the same time, I know that they might recognise their citations, if they do so, I want to make clear that my aim is not to judge anyone. My conclusions arise from my approach to sociology, which I understand as a tool for providing critical analysis of contemporary societies. In my research project I aim to critically describe the experiences of parenting in Poland today from the perspective of gender and economic inequalities. Thus to limit the personal characteristics of interviewed individuals, the citations are signed with pseudonyms and abbreviations, which indicate only gender (W—women, M—men) and family situation (S—single parents, C—coupled parents) of the interviewees and with randomly assigned numbers.

The transcripts of the interviews were analysed in qualitative research software—MaXQDA12. The qualitative analysis of the interviews followed the mixed strategy of thematic and open coding (Ayres 2008; Benaquisto 2008a, b; Gibbs 2011). Initial codes were distinguished based on the theories and themes that appeared during the interviews. Yet during the analysis new codes emerged and were systematically added to the code tree. At the end of the analysis, there were 467 codes, which were assigned to 6690 citations. During the analysis I adopted a strategy of social constructivism, according to which social reality is constructed through human interactions and actions, thus different individuals assign different meanings to different phenomena. These meanings result from their own experiences, but also arise from interactions with other people, in particular family members, friends and co-workers. This also applies to phenomena linked to social inequalities (Harris 2006, 2010). Thus during my analysis of the interviews, I was particularly attentive to meanings and interpretations given by the interviewees. I treated the interviewees as competent actors, who can describe their experiences and the social context in which they function.

## 1.3 Outline of the Book

The book comprises six chapters, including the introduction and conclusion. In this chapter, I present my research project and summarise the methodological choices I made during the collection of data. Chapter 2 is of introductory character, the aim of which is to outline the background for the following analysis. I start with a description of the most important social changes that have had an impact on parenting in contemporary times. I propose to look at parenthood through the lenses of three types of work: care work, paid work and domestic work. Such an approach places some distance from the concept of a work/life balance. I also explain why I decided to use the theoretical perspectives of agency and of *doing gender*. The chapter concludes with analysis of the Polish family policy system, which helps to describe the opportunity structures available to parents living in Poland.

Chapters 3, 4 and 5 are of analytical character and provide analyses of the three types of work: care, paid and domestic. Chapter 3 deals with the issue of care work in the context of care norms and gender beliefs, as well as support from the welfare state. I describe how parents share parental leave in the context of gender inequalities, and how they fill the care gap that results from the incongruency of the parental leave system and institutional care for children. The chapter concludes with a description of the hardship of care work. Chapter 4 is devoted to the organisation of paid work. I argue that paid work is seen as an important obligation resulting from parenthood rather than as an obstacle to it. Then I describe different attitudes to the paid work of men and women before concluding with analysis of time pressures resulting from lack of time. Finally, in Chap. 5 the division of domestic work is studied. I discuss the prevailing gender inequalities in the household and show how, regardless of changing gender roles, men avoid domestic duties while women undertake the role of managers in everyday life. The chapter also presents what strategies parents adopt to reduce the amount of time spent on domestic work and how those strategies are connected to economic inequalities.

In Chap. 6 I attempt to summarise how Polish parents deal with various obligations resulting from care work, paid work and domestic work in the context of gender and economic inequalities. I argue that men and women, as well as individuals with different levels of economic resources, have different opportunity structures, and consequently have different choices available in how they want to organise their everyday life. I argue that the right of choice substantially differs for men and women. The crucial issue here is the power relations in the couple. To describe these power relations I refer to two types of power: *situational power* and *debilitative power*. Then I proceed to the role of the Polish welfare state in reproducing gender and economic inequalities. The chapter concludes with a new set of questions that arose during my research and proposes areas for further studies.

## 1.4 My Contribution

There is a long tradition of sociological study of Polish families. Presently there are many studies conducted on various aspects of family life, including parenting. Yet most of the publications are written in Polish and are not available for a broader audience. Thus my intention was to describe the experience of parenting in contemporary Poland to an English-speaking audience. There is not much research on parenting in post-communist European countries. Most sociological books on parenthood deal with the experiences of parents in Western Europe, whereas I argue here that the experiences of Polish parents are distinctly different. Polish society is still very conservative in terms of gender roles. Owing to low salaries and economic pressures Polish women work full-time in the labour market more often than women in Western Europe. All of this occurs in the context of limited support from the welfare state in institutional care for children. Consequently, gender and economic inequalities are crucial dimensions that need to be taken into consideration when trying to understand the organisation of family life in Polish society. That is why I believe my research can provide a new perspective on parenting in contemporary Europe. The mixed-method approach enables a description of the experience of parenthood in a broader context, and shows how opportunity structures of different parents are created. What is more, analysis through the lenses of three types of work helps to move away from the concept of a work/life balance that has become very prominent in recent decades in family studies.

## References

Ayres, L. (2008). Thematic coding and analysis. In L. M. Given (Ed.), *The SAGE encyclopedia of qualitative research methods* (pp. 867–868). Sage Publications.
Benaquisto, L. (2008a). Code and coding. In L. M. Given (Ed.), *The SAGE encyclopedia of qualitative research methods* (pp. 85–88). Sage Publications.
Benaquisto, L. (2008b). Open coding. In L. M. Given (Ed.), *The SAGE encyclopedia of qualitative research methods* (pp. 581–582). Sage Publications.
Denzin, N. K., & Lincoln, Y. S. (2005). Introduction: The discipline and practice of qualitative research. In N. K. Denzin & Y. S. Lincoln (Eds.), *The SAGE handbook of qualitative research* (3rd ed., pp. 1–32). Sage Publications, Inc..
Gibbs, G. (2011). *Analizowanie danych jakościowych*. Wydawnictwo Naukowe PWN.
Gouldner, A. W. (1970). *The coming crisis of western sociology*. Basic Books.
Harris, S. R. (2006). *The meanings of marital equality*. SUNY Press.
Harris, S. R. (2010). *What is constructionism?: Navigating its use in sociology*. Lynne Rienner Publishers.
Heyink, J. W., & Tymstra, T. J. (1993). The function of qualitative research. *Social Indicators Research, 29*(3), 291–305.
Moran-Ellis, J., Alexander, V. D., Cronin, A., Dickinson, M., Fielding, J., Sleney, J., et al. (2006). Triangulation and integration: Processes, claims and implications. *Qualitative Research, 6*(1), 45–59. https://doi.org/10.1177/1468794106058870.
Rothbauer, P. M. (2008). Triangulation. In L. M. Given (Ed.), *The SAGE encyclopedia of qualitative research methods* (pp. 893–894). Sage Publications.
Saxonberg, S. (2013). From defamilialization to degenderization: Toward a new welfare typology. *Social Policy & Administration, 47*(1), 26–49. https://doi.org/10.1111/j.1467-9515.2012.00836.x.

**Open Access** This chapter is licensed under the terms of the Creative Commons Attribution 4.0 International License (http://creativecommons.org/licenses/by/4.0/), which permits use, sharing, adaptation, distribution and reproduction in any medium or format, as long as you give appropriate credit to the original author(s) and the source, provide a link to the Creative Commons license and indicate if changes were made.

The images or other third party material in this chapter are included in the chapter's Creative Commons license, unless indicated otherwise in a credit line to the material. If material is not included in the chapter's Creative Commons license and your intended use is not permitted by statutory regulation or exceeds the permitted use, you will need to obtain permission directly from the copyright holder.

# Chapter 2
# Parenting, Gender and Work: A Sociological Perspective

**Abstract** This chapter presents the issue of parenthood as a subject of sociological inquiry in the context of broader social and cultural changes. I demonstrate why parenthood should be perceived as a process that is strictly connected with social, cultural and institutional contexts. Keeping this in mind I argue that there is no one proper way of doing parenthood. The most important aspect here are the links between parenthood and paid work. I critically approach the concept of work/life balance that is vastly popular in contemporary social sciences, but in my opinion is not always adequate to describe parenting in a post-communist society. I propose to look at parenthood through the lenses of three types of work: care work, paid work and domestic work. I claim that such approach helps to grasp different ways of parenting in contemporary times, as well as to recognise persisting gender and economic inequalities.

**Keywords** Parenthood · Parenting · Poland · Care work · Paid work · Domestic work

## 2.1 Introduction

The experience of parenting is widespread for most people who lived in the twentieth century and are living at the beginning of the twenty-first century. As demographic analysis shows, throughout industrialised societies only 10–20% of people remained childless. In Europe the lowest proportion of childless people is characteristic for the cohorts born in 1930s, 1940s and 1950s. In Poland only 10% of women born between 1950 and 1954 remained childless (Rowland 2007). Yet even though in younger cohorts (born after 1960) researchers have observed increasing childlessness in European countries, the proportion of childless women rarely exceeded 20% (Sobotka 2017). In the Central and Eastern European (CEE) region the share of childless cohorts is the lowest in Europe (5–15%) for cohorts born between 1900s and 1970s. This data indicates that being a parent is an experience shared by at least 75% of people in older generations. Other studies also indicate that younger generations are willing to become parents—for example in Poland in 2011 only 12% of childless people aged between 18 and 39 do not want to have children at all (Kotowska 2014; Mynarska 2011). All of this suggests that most people in contemporary Western societies experience or will experience parenting during their lifetime. Thus the issue of parenting is highly important for sociologists. It can be assumed that parenting greatly affects the organisation of people's everyday life and society in general.

What is the sociological definition of parenthood then? There is no simple answer to this question. First of all, there is a need to distinguish between parenting and parenthood. To do so, I refer to the distinctions proposed by Tina Miller in her two books, one on motherhood (2005) and one on fatherhood (2011), in which she clarifies that mothering and fathering refer to personal experiences mothers and fathers have in their lives, whereas motherhood and fatherhood are defined in a wider societal context as constructed categories which indicate what individuals as mothers and fathers should do. Parenting is a personal experience of individuals that takes place in the context of parenthood models which define parents' roles and obligations. So even though parenting is a biological phenomenon, which results from a human being's biological ability to reproduce, it is not a homogeneous experience for all individuals. The ways people realise their role as a parent are diversified and differ between various societies and cultures, between historical periods, as well as between men and women, people from different social classes, living in different places, having different family situations and so on. In this book I concentrate mostly on parenting, so on parents' practices and experiences that take place in a particular social, cultural and institutional context, i.e. in Polish society at the beginning of the twenty-first century. The models of motherhood and fatherhood together with gender beliefs are an important background, which highly influence the way men and women practice parenting.

## 2.2 Parenting and Social Changes

Parenting today is strictly linked with the broader organisation of family life and work. To describe contemporary times sociologists often use the term 'late modernity'. Late modernity is characterised by rapid and constant changes of social reality, as well as uncertainty and ambiguity (Giddens 1991). As Krystyna Slany underlines, in the new theories of contemporary times transformations are described in at least four dimensions: (1) technological changes linked with science and knowledge; (2) economic changes affecting the organisation of work and production; (3) social changes resulting from new social movements, in particular the feminist movement and the sexual revolution, which altered models of family, marriage and other social relations; (4) cultural changes with which new norms, values, ideologies and identities appeared (Slany 2002, pp. 24–25). In the context of this book social and cultural changes are the most important, since they have mostly affected the prevailing models of motherhood and fatherhood and have led to renegotiation of the contract between men and women. Yet economic changes have also had an impact on how parents function today—where they work, for how long, how (in)-secure they feel in the labour market, what they can afford, where they live and so on. All of these have an impact on how men and women engage in their parental roles and how they experience parenting.

One of the most salient characteristics for contemporary times is changes in the organisation of family life. In the twentieth century we can observe the diversification of family living arrangements that have resulted from demographic change, including longer life expectancy, postponed marriage and childbearing, increased number of children born outside marriage, decreasing fertility rates, growing number of single parents, cohabitation, divorce, as well as remarriage (Kimmel 2011; Slany 2002, 2013; van Eeden-Moorefield and Demo 2007). Besides there are *new* arrangements of parenting, which are no longer only performed by biological mothers and fathers, but also by adoptive parents, parents living with new partners (step-parents), and parents living in nonheterosexual or polyamorous relationships (Balzarini et al. 2019; Mizielińska 2017; Mizielińska et al. 2014). All these changes are described against the backdrop of a *traditional* nuclear family model, in which men and women play specific roles and live together with their children in one household. Such a model is often treated as the ideal, and all the above-mentioned changes are treated as a sign of *family crisis*. Yet, as historians and sociologists have noted, this *ideal* model is a relatively new historical development that appeared together with industrial societies, it was also a social phenomenon limited to particular geographical locations and particular social classes (Flandrin 1979; Kimmel 2011; Mizielińska 2017; Szlendak 2011; Żurek 2020). Therefore, as sociologists we should be cautious with strong claims about family crisis, since they derive more from a normative ideal of a family than historical facts (Giza-Poleszczuk 2005). Family life, as other aspects of social reality, is under constant change and it is hard to find any stable elements in it (Elias 1978, 2000). Thus in this book parenting and models of parenthood are seen in terms of processes that are fluid and open to constant transformation. I assume that there is no one proper way of doing parenthood as individuals change during their life courses and their parenting practices change over time.

The ways men and women engage in parenting are strongly linked with the changing reality of late modernity, as well as with normative ideals of how a family and its members should function. Yet they are also connected to the economic dimension of social reality. Karl Marx and Friedrich Engels (Engels 1884/2010; Marx and Engels 1848/1969) underlined the link between prevailing family models based on gender inequalities and the economic system. In capitalist societies the single family is an economic unit within which there is a particular division of work and production. Women are dependent on men who have to engage in paid work to support their families. Family ties among workers are 'transformed into simple articles of commerce and instruments of labour' (Marx and Engels 1848/1969). The world described by Marx and Engels is of course characteristic of a different historical period, yet also today the organisation of family life is strictly connected to the economy and the organisation of labour. That is why it is impossible to analyse contemporary parenting without taking into consideration the working situation of parents. Today global competitive capitalism affects the everyday life of every individual. On the one hand, the European Union from the very beginning has promoted a high level of employment. In the Europe 2020 strategy the goal was set to increase the labour market participation of people aged 20–64 to 75% by 2020. Many social benefits are connected with employment. This basically means that the European welfare states expect almost everyone to work in the labour market. In the capitalist world paid work is seen as an instrument of earning income that is necessary to live and consume (Chang 2014). Paid work is supposed to protect individuals from poverty and homelessness. Yet at the same time the conditions of paid work are far from perfect. Individuals in the labour market face precarious working conditions, low salaries and even potential job loss, as well as working hours which are either too long or too short. Sometimes they have to migrate to other places, even to other countries, seeking work. Women and people from different minority groups have to deal with discrimination in the labour market (Standing 2014; Tomescu-Dubrow et al. 2019; Wrench et al. 2016). In the context of parenthood, this means that parents are at risk of various processes resulting from competitive capitalism.

The tensions between parenthood and work are rather well described in the social sciences (Bäck-Wiklund et al. 2011; Crespi and Ruspini 2016; Drobnič and Guillén 2011; Olah and Frątczak 2013; Spitzmueller and Matthews 2016). In particular the welfare state is present in contemporary discussions on parenting. The role of welfare states that appeared in the twentieth century is to protect their citizens, especially those who are the most vulnerable and face problems with fulfilling basic human needs, but also those who just participate in the labour market. The welfare state should guarantee the right to work in proper conditions, as well as the right to an income. Yet in this context the welfare state also addresses the issue of family and family obligations (Esping-Andersen 1990, 2002). In contemporary European countries we are all accustomed to the idea of paid or unpaid maternity or parental leave, public childcare institutions, child benefit, a public education system and public healthcare. All of these elements of the state are designed to assist individuals in their family obligations. Therefore, today the welfare state plays an important role in how family life is organised and how particular individuals engage in parental obligations. On the one hand, its role should be to protect and assist individuals in their parenting practices, but on the other hand, its instruments are far from ideal and are often based on tacit assumptions about preferable family models and/or gender roles which promote and support particular parenting practices whilst ignoring or opposing others.

## 2.3 Parenting as Work from a Sociological Perspective

Keeping in mind all the above mentioned issues, parenting is analysed in this book by taking into consideration the various aspects and different contexts within which it occurs. My aim is to provide a critical sociological description of parenting in

## 2.3 Parenting as Work from a Sociological Perspective

contemporary times based on the example of Polish society. I claim here that the critical approach requires distancing from the construct of a work/life balance that has become one of the most common theoretical tools to analyse the experiences of parenting in contemporary capitalist societies. I argue that the theoretical construct of a work/life balance is normative and based on several hidden assumptions that do not allow for an adequate and critical analysis of parenting experiences today. These assumptions are not value free, but promote a particular 'permitted world', using Alvin Gouldner's concept (1970), that is regarded as a desirable and 'normal' way of being a parent. What is more, the concept is vague and ill defined, since it is not clear what *work*, *life* and *balance* really indicate. I have identified six hidden assumptions of the work/life balance construct, which are as follows:

1. There is an obvious boundary set between the area of work and non-work activities in everyday life.
2. Only paid work in the labour market is recognised as work, therefore in an ideal world everybody should be engaged in paid work. Those who do not engage in paid work never work.
3. Unpaid work in the domestic sphere is not perceived as work, and as such it is not perceived as an activity oriented on the production of goods and services. Consequently, it is perceived as being less significant than paid work in the labour market.
4. Everyone is expected to be in paid employment or at least seek it.
5. Everyone is expected to have a family and sustain family relationships.
6. Everyone should combine paid work with family life and find some satisfaction with this combination.

Since the construct is prevalent and often adopted to analyse parenting today, I propose to start thinking about parenting in terms of various types of work, rather than something that is in collision with work (in particular paid work). I am convinced that such an approach would better serve sociologists for providing an adequate and critical description of social reality. To do this there is a need to get rid of thinking in terms of work and life as two opposite elements in individuals' lives. Work is an important element of people' lives and as such should not be treated as something distinctive, but rather as a crucial element of individual lives in capitalist societies.

Furthermore, there is a need to recognise different types of work. According to sociological definitions, work is understood as activities involved in the production of goods and services in order to cater to one's own needs (Bonstead-Bruns 2007; Reskin 2000). Yet even though this definition indicates that work is not necessarily done for pay, in analysis regarding the work/life balance it is implicitly assumed that work means paid work done in the labour market. Sociologists tend to overlook unpaid work done in the household, as well as volunteer work. Unpaid work done outside the labour market is often invisible (Oakley 2018; Reskin 2000; Tancred 1995; Zachorowska-Mazurkiewicz 2016). At the same time, it is an important aspect of people's everyday life, especially in the context of family life. As Anna Zachorowska-Mazurkiewicz (2017, p. 121) notes 'unpaid labour and care are important sources of comfort and support in people's daily lives.' She further observes that without this type of labour people would not be able to survive either as individuals or as society. The importance of unpaid work was originally recognised by second-wave feminist scholars over four decades ago (Hochschild and Machung 2003; Oakley 2018; Tancred 1995). The invisibility of unpaid work resulted from the process of industrialisation that has led to an increasing number of people who work outside the household for pay, consequently the division on paid work in the labour market and work done at home for catering to individuals' needs was established. These changes took place simultaneously with a growing specialisation in social roles and social relations, as well as growing consumption (Zachorowska-Mazurkiewicz 2017). The division of paid and unpaid work overlaps with a division of male and female obligations. The process of industrialisation strengthened gender inequality in everyday life. In the ideal model men were responsible to economically provide for their families, whereas a woman's obligation was to take care of household duties and children. In fact this division was of a moral character rather than an instrumental one, since many women actively participated in the labour market. Under such conditions work was defined as 'a paid economic activity linked to the market' and all other kinds of work done outside the market were ignored (Zachorowska-Mazurkiewicz 2017, p. 122). Yet, as feminist scholars argue, such an approach is not accurate, since it does not recognise the importance of unpaid work for the whole of society. Peta Tancred, using the concept of the 'productive and reproductive spheres' to describe the division of paid and unpaid work, argues that these two spheres are greatly intertwined: 'the whole nature of the productive sphere is based on the premise that someone else is looking after the reproductive sphere' (Tancred 1995, p. 14). In other words, without reproductive work in the household, it would be difficult to fully engage in paid work in the labour market.

Thus it is necessary to distinguish different types of work. In the context of parenting in contemporary European societies there are three basic categories: (1) *care work* done in connection to having children (and other dependent family members), (2) *paid work* done in the labour market and (3) *domestic work* done in the household. All of them are connected to each other. As I shall show in the following chapters, sometimes there is a problem with finding a clear boundary between them. Yet there are several reasons why it is convenient to keep to these categories. First, parenthood is a highly gendered phenomenon. The division of traditional maternal and paternal duties often overlaps with the division of paid and unpaid work—men are mainly responsible for breadwinning, whereas women's obligation is to take care of children and deal with housework. When analysing different types of work separately, we can clearly see inequalities between men and women. Secondly, the transition to parenthood is connected to great changes in an individual's life, as well as family life in general. As much research shows, transition to parenthood is often associated with an increasing number of care and domestic obligations, this requires rethinking issues of paid work—such as the length of working hours, time of work, taking longer leave and so on. For many people it is only after becoming parents that they start to experience time conflict or more

## 2.3 Parenting as Work from a Sociological Perspective

critically assess their attitudes to paid work. Thirdly, it is important to recognise the difference between care work and domestic work. Of course, in many cases they overlap, yet at the same time they significantly differ, interviewees from my research recognised this difference. Even though care work is present to some extent in everyone's life, childless people usually have a lot fewer care obligations than parents. This is because care of children, especially small ones, requires constant attention and in many situations cannot be totally transferred to other people—of course parents can share care work with others, for example babysitters, grandparents, childcare institutions, yet they are still solely responsible for how this care is arranged. This responsibility is ever-present. Care work is imbued with greater emotional engagement than domestic work, which, whilst having its own importance, requires less attention and can be postponed or more easily transferred to other people. Finally, such a categorisation of work allows for comparisons between different studies on parenthood. There are studies that concentrate on the issue of the work/life balance, in such studies researchers usually focus on paid work in the labour market and analyse how people combine this with other parental obligations. They usually refer, implicitly or explicitly, to such a division (Crespi and Ruspini 2016; Drobnič and Guillén 2011; Lewis et al. 2017; Olah and Frątczak 2013). There are other studies that concentrate on everyday parental obligations connected to care work, organisation of everyday practices with children, as well as relations between parents and children (Doucet 2004; Miller 2005, 2011; Sikorska 2019). There are many studies that deal with these issues in the context of migration (Pustułka et al. 2015; Ślusarczyk 2019; Urbańska 2015, 2016). Finally, there are studies which analyse the organisation of domestic work, unpaid work done in the household, which is highly gendered, but the organisation of which differs depending on social class, economic situation, location of residence and level of engagement with the welfare system (Boje 2006; Coltrane 2000; Greenstein 2009; Schober 2013; Titkow et al. 2004; Warren 2003).

In my analysis of parenting, I concentrate on the issue of work, that which is either done at home or for pay. This focus on work results from the fact that at the beginning my aim was to identify the strategies used by Polish parents for achieving a work/life balance. Yet during the fieldwork and analysis of the data, I realised that the concept of a work/life balance is not very useful. This concept is restraining and often inadequate to describe the situation of many parents, especially those who do not fit to the *ideal* model of two employed, middle-class parents with healthy kids. To move away from this concept whilst still using the collected data, I decided to distinguish the most important elements of parenting experiences in contemporary Poland. I concentrated on the issue of work, since the interviewed parents talked about this topic most. Yet I am aware that parenting is something more than only work.

## 2.4 Parenting and Doing Gender

Parenting is a social and cultural phenomenon, it is not only determined by the biological features of human bodies, but rather results from various norms, social expectations and prevailing models of behaviour in a particular society. It has not always been obvious for sociologists and social scientists to analyse parenthood as a social construct. As a gendered phenomenon people often confuse biological predispositions of men and women with cultural and social expectations grounded in norms and values. A good example of such confusion is the functionalist perspective in sociology, in which it is assumed that in modern societies models of motherhood and fatherhood are based on distinctive, yet complementary, obligations (Bales and Parsons 1955; Parsons 1955; Zelditch 1955). Functionalists treat the nuclear family as a subsystem and analyse it in terms of its functions. They indicate two characteristics that determine the role of individuals within the family: sex and age. The first function of the nuclear family is the socialisation of children, in which children learn how to function in a society and what values are important. The second function is important from the perspective of adults—marriage and becoming a parent are significant events in an individual's life, which are necessary to achieve an emotional balance. The roles in marriage and the family are based on an instrumental/expressive axis and are related to the occupational system. In modern societies the family does not produce all necessary products and services by itself, but can function thanks to external economic income gained by family members' participation in the external occupational system. That is why there is a need to differentiate roles in the family—one person focuses on economic provisions for the whole family, whereas the second is responsible for emotional stability and takes care of family relations. In this division men participate in the occupational system, whereas women are responsible for the domestic sphere. The difference between men and women is described here as functional, and is explained with biological differences between genders—women because of their ability to become pregnant and breastfeed *naturally* belong to a domestic sphere and have predispositions to take care of relations between family members. This does not mean that in the functionalist perspective women's work in the labour market is not recognised—it is, yet it is never recognised as a primary role—women are expected to resign from paid work in connection with motherhood. Even though the functionalist perspective is formulated to make it appear unbiased and objective, it is in fact based on the false premise that men and women are distinctly different, and that this is a result of biological differences between male and female bodies. At the same time, the nuclear family described by functionalism is a very limited social phenomenon, which was characteristic for middle-class families living in the United States in the 1950s. As Michael Kimmel notes:

> The so-called traditional system of dads who head out to work every morning, leaving moms to stay at home with the children as full-time housewives and mothers, was an invention of the 1950s – and part of a larger ideological effort to facilitate the re-entry of American men

## 2.4 Parenting and Doing Gender

back into the workplace and domestic life after World War II and to legitimate the return of women from the workplace and back into the home. (2011, p. 248)

The confusions of biological and cultural predispositions of men and women to parenting are grounded in a broader system of gender inequalities. The dimension of gender inequality is crucial for my analysis. To understand how contemporary societies function it is necessary to analyse gender relations and how they affect the everyday lives of men and women. Family is one of the most important and the most resilient of social institutions, at the same time it is also one of the most gendered ones. This means that the functioning of the family is strictly connected to gender roles and unequal gender relations. In this book parenting is analysed in terms of work, as activities that are undertaken to cater to one's own needs. Consequently, to describe the experiences of Polish parents, I refer here to the theoretical approach of *doing gender* proposed by Candace West and Don H. Zimmerman (1987, 2009), in which gender is perceived as an ongoing situated process, in which masculinity and femininity are not ascribed, but rather achieved and connected to a particular system of relationships. Gender then is interactional and institutional, it is also subject to constant social change (West and Zimmerman 2009). Furthermore, in the context of this book, it is important that gender is also relational—the scripts of being a man and a woman refer to each other, as well as to the broader dominant models of masculinity and femininity. In this approach, gender is not perceived as an individual characteristic, but rather 'an emergent property of social situations: both an outcome of and a rationale for various social arrangements and a means of justifying one of the most fundamental divisions of society' (West and Fenstermaker 1995, p. 9).

Despite decades of the feminist movement, gender inequalities still persist today. Family life, especially parenthood, is one of those areas in which these inequalities are particularly visible. As research shows, the transition to parenthood results in re-traditionalisation of how everyday life is organised—women undertake more domestic and care duties while reducing their engagement in paid work (Paull 2008; Schober 2013; Solera and Mencarini 2018; van der Lippe et al. 2011). This means that the consequences of becoming a parent are different for men and women, and that parenthood reinforces gender inequalities. In the context of the three types of work connected to parenthood distinguished above—care, paid and domestic— the theoretical perspective of doing gender helps to explain the parenting experiences of men and women. These experiences are not only a result of individual choices made by parents, but are also strictly connected with the social, cultural and institutional contexts which characterise the particular acceptable models of mothering and fathering. These models serve as a reference point for individuals as they engage in their parental roles. They are an important element of gender beliefs, which can be defined as 'the cultural rules or instructions for enacting the social structure of difference and inequality that we understand to be gender' (Ridgeway and Correll 2004, p. 511). Their role is twofold—on the one hand, they specify how men and women should behave in particular situations, on the other hand, they serve as a set of rules which allows the behaviour of others to be evaluated (Ridgeway and Correll 2004).

In family life, especially parenthood, it is especially difficult to ignore gender beliefs and to undo gender. This is because parenthood is not only a cultural and social phenomenon, but it also has a biological dimension. Consequently, the differences between a mother and a father are often perceived in terms of biological differences between female and male bodies—the first one is capable of childbearing and breastfeeding, whereas the latter is deprived of these abilities. The role of a mother is thus defined at the beginning, since she was pregnant, gave birth and then breastfed a child. During this time the role of a father is only one of being supportive. As I showed in my research on fatherhood, these initial differences between a mother and a father resulting from biological differences serve as an explanation for the diversification of maternal and paternal obligations at the later stage of being a parent (Suwada 2015, 2017a). Consequently, women remain as the primary caregiver, whereas men are rather perceived in terms of secondary caregiver or a helper whose role is to support the mother in everyday life. His primary obligation is to provide economically for his family. This differentiation of a mother's or father's obligation has consequences for the organisation of work within the family. Paid work in the labour market is perceived as being more of a male duty. Care and domestic work remain as a woman's duty to perform or at least manage.

In contemporary times even though sociologists observe the increasing participation of women in the labour market, as well as the increasing involvement of fathers in care and domestic obligations, there are still great inequalities within the household. They are, on the one hand, connected with gender beliefs affecting the way individuals think about motherhood and fatherhood, but on the other hand they are also strictly connected with the institutional context, i.e. the organisation of the labour market, the welfare state, and in particular family policy. These institutional settings can reinforce or weaken gender beliefs about the level of engagement in parenthood of mothers and fathers. In the next part of the chapter, I shall concentrate on this issue more carefully.

## 2.5 Parenting and the Welfare State

Gender beliefs are an important element of the gender system based on inequalities between men and women. They are not only important for individuals and how they behave in everyday life, but they are also an important point of reference in designing the family policy system. At the beginning of the twenty-first century parenthood is a political concern. This is not only because of the feminist movement and feminist scholars who recognised that 'the personal is political', questioned the division on public and private spheres, and showed how the everyday life of women is embedded in the broader structure of gender inequalities (Hanisch 2006; Rogan and Budgeon 2018), but also because family life was recognised as a sphere affected

## 2.5 Parenting and the Welfare State

by the public sphere, in particular the organisation of the labour market and family policy system.

The family policy system is aimed at supporting parents in reconciling parenting obligations with paid work in the labour market. Therefore, when analysing the parenting experience today we need to look not only at individual motivations and actions, but also on the structures created by social, economic and political conditions. The general point of theoretical reference in this book is the concept of agency that attempts to explain the links between individual behaviours at the microlevel of a particular society with its macrostructures. Anne Lisa Ellingsæter and Lars Gulbrandsen, referring to a concept of agency, claim that 'social action is an outcome of a choice within constraints, and preferences underlying choice are shaped by the constraints' (Ellingsæter and Gulbrandsen 2007, p. 656). Thus individuals function in a social reality that limits their actions. Such a social reality can be understood as *opportunity structures*, which in the case of parents determine their everyday practices (Ellingsæter and Gulbrandsen 2007; Javornik and Kurowska 2017). The family policy system is an important element shaping the opportunity structures of parents. In particular, it affects the way parents can or cannot fulfil various obligations resulting from being a parent, in this book I am especially interested in how the family policy system shapes the opportunities of parents to combine paid work, care work and domestic work.

Research on the welfare state indicates that various family policy systems differently affect people's everyday life. In this book I concentrate on the Polish family system that is an example of a post-communist system and has many common features with systems of other countries from Central and Eastern Europe. To map the opportunity structures that the Polish system creates in the case of Polish parents, I refer to the historical-institutional analysis of Steven Saxonberg (2014), who claims that post-communist Europe is characterised by gendering family policies. Consequently, 'it seems clear that the policies pursued have not enabled women to balance work and family life, and that in fact they have led to a large drop in fertility rates' (Saxonberg 2014, p. 33). The analysis of Saxonberg is based on his welfare state typology regarding the dimension of genderisation-degenderisation (2013). In this typology the crucial question is how particular policies reinforce or reconstruct traditional gender roles. Looking at the welfare state in the context of its impact on gender relations has a long tradition in feminist studies (Connell 2009; Giullari and Lewis 2005; Orloff 1996, 2009). It is recognised that the links between gender relations and the welfare state is twofold. On the one hand, states can support the social reproduction or reconstruction of gender order based on inequalities. On the other hand, changing gender relations have an impact on the character of the welfare state (Orloff 1996). For my analysis the crucial question is how the institutional system of family policy affects gender relations within the family and shapes opportunity structures of mothers and fathers in the context of three types of work: paid work, care work and domestic work. To answer this question it is necessary to distinguish the most important instruments of the family policy system and recognise their impact on the everyday organisation of parents' lives.

The Polish family policy system is based on three main instruments: (1) parental leave, (2) institutional care for children, and (3) cash benefits. All these elements went through significant reform in the first and second decades of the twenty-first century. Below I try to briefly describe these three elements and depict the opportunity structures of Polish parents in 2017. Since the in-depth interviews on which the following analysis is based were conducted in 2017, I shall concentrate on how the system looked up to 2017, even though since them some elements have been changed (for example in cash benefits and in the number of places in care institutions available for children under three). Since there are many analyses of how the system has changed in the last two decades, I focus only on the institutional settings in which the interviewed parents functioned. The sample only included parents whose youngest child was no older than eight. Thus I am particularly interested in how the system was designed 2009–2017.

In the 2010s the system of parental leave went through significant reforms. Parents of children born in 2010 had a right to 20 weeks of maternity leave, two weeks of additional maternity leave and one week of paternity leave (all paid at 100% salary). In 2012 the additional maternity leave was prolonged to four weeks and paternity leave to two weeks. In 2013 the system went through the most significant reform—a new type of leave was introduced called parental leave, it was 26 weeks long. Also in 2013 additional maternity leave was extended to 6 weeks. Consequently, at that time parents had a right to 20 weeks of maternity leave, 6 weeks of additional maternity leave and 26 weeks of parental leave (together 52 weeks, which is almost one year). Since the system was a bit confusing for many parents, in 2016 the additional maternity leave was integrated with parental leave, so from then on parents could use 20 weeks of maternity leave and 32 weeks of parental leave. The replacement rate in these leaves is high—if parents plan to use all 52 weeks then a person on leave gets 80% of their salary, if they plan to use only 26 weeks, the replacement rate is 100%, in such cases all additional weeks are paid at 60%. Through all these years after using maternity and parental leave parents could also take advantage of a three-year-long extended leave, which is means-tested—the benefit being 400 PLN per month (ca. 90 euros) is paid only to parents not exceeding income criterion 500 PLN per person per month in the household. In this case, for most parents this type of leave is unpaid.

As in the case with most post-communist countries in Europe, institutional care for children in Poland is a two-tier system, in which there are nurseries for children under three and preschools for children aged three–six years. Even though this division has its roots in the nineteenth century in the Austrian Empire (for more details see: Saxonberg 2014), it still persists in the Polish system and has consequences for the enrolment rates of children under or over three years. Today the Polish system for the institutional care of children is a mixture of public and private institutions. In 2017 72% of nurseries were private, but they offered only 52.8% of all available places. Yet since private institutions are also subsidised by the state, 86% of all children in public and private nurseries benefited from partial or total funding by the municipality (Statistics Poland 2018). According to Statistics Poland, in 2017 only 8.6% of children under three were enrolled at a care institution (13.3%

in cities and 2% in rural areas). Whereas the enrolment rates for children aged three–six were 86.4% in general (99.9% in cities and 67.9% in rural areas). The lack of places in care institutions for children under three is one of the greatest challenges for Polish policy-makers. Since 2011 the program 'Toddler' has been implemented, which aims to increase the number of available places. Poland is also obliged by the European Union to increase the enrolment rates of children under three to at least 33% (European Commission 2013). So even though since 2011 enrolment rates have risen from 3.8% to 10.5%, in 2018 there was still a huge unsatisfied care demand for the youngest children. As I show in the following chapters, the experiences of parents also indicate that there is a huge problem with organising care for children under three.

The last element of the family policy system is child benefit. This universal cash benefit is a fairly new instrument for Polish parents, it was introduced in 2016 by the programme 'Family 500+'. The benefit is an untaxed 500 PLN per month for a child. Initially, this benefit was restricted to families with more than one child—parents received the benefit for every second and following child. In the case of one-child families, the benefit was means-tested and was available for parents whose income per person in a household was not higher than 800 PLN per month (or in the case of children with disabilities not higher than 1200 PLN per month). In July 2019 the programme was extended and now every parent has a right to this benefit regardless of the number of children or the financial situation of the family.[1] Additionally, parents have a right to tax relief in connection with having children, there is also a system of financial aid for the poorest families. Even though the aim of the 'Family 500+' programme was to increase fertility rates by financial support for families, the instrument is often perceived as redirecting women away from the labour market and into motherhood (Gromada 2017; Ruzik-Sierdzińska 2017).

The Polish family policy system is grounded on traditional and conservative views about gender roles and the organisation of family life. Dorota Szelewa (2017) notes that post-1989 evolution of the Polish welfare state is characterised by the state's withdrawal from the social policy programme. In family policy this was connected primarily with spending cuts on formal care. Thus after 1989 the Polish family policy system engaged in a process of re-familialisation, and was defined as 'implicit familialism', in which the lack of support from the state meant putting the burden of care on families, in particular women. Yet the beginning of the twenty-first century is a time of greater focus on family policy. As Szelewa indicates, in 2005 a conservative government took office and started a transition towards explicit familialism that finalised in 2015 with the introduction of the 'Family 500+' programme. As Sigrid Leitner argues 'the explicit familialism not only strengthens the family in caring for children, the handicapped and the elderly through familial policies. It also lacks the provision of any alternative to family

---

[1]As the interviews were conducted before the 'Family 500+' programme was extended to include the first born child, all parents in the research had experience of its earlier restricted version. Yet some of them were also eligible to receive the benefit for their first child.

care. This lack in public and market driven care provision together with strong familialization explicitly enforces the caring function of the family' (2003, pp. 358–359). The greater focus on cash benefits than on childcare institutions could be evidence of adopting explicit familialism by Polish policy-makers. Even though in the Polish system there are some elements of public and private care institutions, especially for children over three years, it is clear that the current government puts more pressure on familial rhetoric and traditional gender roles and does not guarantee a stable funding for childcare institutions.

The process of re-familialisation that has been taking place since 1989 has great consequences for women and prevailing gender inequalities. The concepts of familialisation and defamilialisation are at risk of adopting gender neutrality and not recognising that putting the burden of care and domestic work on the family in fact usually means putting it on women. Thus to better understand what consequences the familial orientation of the Polish family policy system has on opportunity structures of men and women, I refer to the previously mentioned concepts of genderisation and degenderisation. Saxonberg (2013) distinguishes three types of policies based on the axis of genderisation/degenderisation. On the one hand, there are policies that are degenderising, and their aim is to support the elimination of traditional gender roles. On the other hand, there are genderising policies, which promote the different roles of men and women in relation to family life and labour market participation. Referring to a difference proposed by Leitner (2003) between implicitly and explicitly familialising policies, Saxonberg recognises implicitly and explicitly genderising policies. The explicitly genderising policies openly support the traditional gender order and family roles in the family, whereas implicitly genderising policies simply ignore the gender dimension and through gender neutrality contribute to the reproduction of gender unequal societies. Keeping in mind the three main instruments of family policy, the Polish system can be defined as explicitly genderising. The parental leave system in particular is openly oriented to women and does not recognise fathers as its main recipients. Even though in 2013 the new leave which was introduced was formulated in gender neutral terms (highly paid 26 weeks of parental leave, in 2016 extended to 32 weeks) the policy-makers did not decide to encourage men to actually use it. Parental leave from the very beginning was perceived as an extension of maternity leave and was perceived mostly as a mother's right that in some special circumstances could be transferred to fathers (for more details see: Suwada 2017a, b). Consequently, in the Polish system only women are expected to take longer breaks in connection to parenthood. Men's care obligations are ignored by the system.

The way institutional care for children is designed in Poland also has genderising consequences for women. The lack of places in institutions for children under three creates particularly difficult conditions for women. After 52 weeks of highly paid maternity and parental leave, parents need to organise care for their children. The interviewees' experiences show that the period between the end of paid leave and the time when a child can go to preschool when they are three can be very problematic. I call this period a *care gap*, since there are no good mechanisms that help parents in organising care. The system gives parents three possibilities: (1) finding a place in a nursery, which is very hard because of lack of places, this is especially so in smaller towns and rural areas; (2) taking an extended parental leave, which is unpaid or low-paid and requires a longer break from paid work, this type of leave is only available to one of the parents, which in practice usually means the mother; (3) hiring a nanny, which even though it can be subsidised by the state, is still very expensive and unaffordable for most parents. In Chap. 3 I show how parents deal with this care gap in everyday life. The institutional conditions create a situation in which there is a great pressure on women to resign from paid work or at least reduce working hours for this period of time. This pressure is reinforced by the cultural norms around care. An important context in Polish society is *the idea of threeness*, according to which mothers should take care of their children until they are three years old. This is connected with a conviction that it is better for child development to be at home with a mother until three years than to spend this time in care institutions.

Paradoxically, this norm is not a reason why there is a division of nurseries and preschools in Poland today. This has its origins in the institutional context of the Austrian Empire (then the Austro-Hungarian Empire) in the nineteenth century. Today on its territory there are four countries: Hungary, Slovakia, Czechia and part of Poland. All of these countries developed a two-tier system based on the division of institutions for children under or above three years of age (Saxonberg 2014). Saxonberg et al. (2012) argue that the idea of threeness is an example of how institutions can influence discourses.

> The idea of threeness actually came from the Lutheran Church [...]. They thought that the main task of preschools was to ingrain children at an early age into Protestant religious values, including obedience and the Protestant work ethic. Thus, the division of children above and below three did not emerge from any kind of modern psychological research on child development, but rather it came about from century old beliefs about the age at which children were ripe for learning certain religious values. The roots of threeness have nothing to do with the issue as to whether it is good for mothers to stay at home with their children during the first three years. (2012, pp. 10–11)

In the Polish case, nurseries were never very popular, especially because of the strong influence of the Catholic church, which defended the family as a private institution. Consequently, even though nurseries were an element of the family policy system for the whole of the twentieth century, the system was never highly developed and enrolment rates were always rather low in comparison to other countries in the region (Saxonberg 2014). Yet the idea of threeness is still very dominant today in Polish society, it is reinforced by a system which provides insufficient nurseries places and in which hiring a nanny is impossibly expensive for most parents. Consequently, there is a pressure on a mother to provide care for her children until they are three years old, this is so even if she works full-time. There is no similar pressure on fathers. To understand this difference in attitudes towards men and women in connection with parenthood in Polish society it is important to refer to another cultural norm. In Polish society there is a strong myth of *Matka Polka* (*the Polish mother*) according to which a woman's role is to devote herself to childbearing and childrearing for the sake of her country. The figure of *Matka Polka* was particularly strong when Poland lacked independence, and also when Polish men were fighting wars in the nineteenth and twentieth centuries. As Anna Titkow notes (2012), this figure legitimised a woman's position of power in the family.

> Difficult life conditions led to a special variety of matriarchy, characteristic for the communist and post-communist states of the Eastern Europe. Matriarchy, in which laden with shopping bags, often experiencing lack of sleep, a terribly tired woman also has a justified sense of being an irreplaceable manager of family life, fulfilling countless duties and tasks.[2] (Titkow 2012, p. 33)

This special position of a mother in the family was a reason why women accepted inequality—'in a system where the state tried to exert totalitarian control over society, the family was the one space in which people felt secure – able to be their *true* selves and to express their true opinions. Women often *wanted* to have the main responsibility for the family' (Saxonberg 2014, p. 45). Consequently, as many researchers have observed, men in communist Poland did not hold the traditional male role as head of their household. They were rather remote, they belonged to the labour market and their role was limited to breadwinning. This situation is still visible today—in Polish families a father is often absent and lacking agency in everyday family life (Marody and Giza-Poleszczuk 2000; Saxonberg 2014; Stanisz 2014).

The concept of opportunity structures allows us to see how the institutional and social as well as cultural contexts shape the situation of individual human beings. The Polish institutional system together with cultural norms about care creates strikingly different opportunity structures for men and women in a situation of parenthood. Women are expected to take longer breaks from employment in connection to parenthood, they are overwhelmed with a double burden plus the lack of institutional support which primarily affects their everyday life. They experience more so called *combination pressures*, which result from the combination of often conflicting expectations resulting from family life and paid work (van der Lippe et al. 2006). At the same time, men are mostly expected to concentrate on paid work and provide for their families. They are not even encouraged to use parental leave and they deal differently with the consequences of the institutional care gap. What is more, since expectations from men in connection to childcare are limited, they do not experience combination pressures in the same way as women. Although, as my following analysis shows they also experience difficulties in being a parent.

## 2.6 Conclusion

From a sociological perspective, parenthood is one of the most important experiences that the majority of people share. To understand how society works it is necessary to recognise how people fulfil their parental obligations. In contemporary times the links between parenthood and paid work seem to be core areas of interest

---

[2]All citations from the Polish publications are translated by the author.

for the welfare state. In the following analysis, my aim is to describe the experience of parenting in Polish society at the beginning of the twenty-first century. Yet I shift away from the popular concept of a work/life balance that, as I argue, is not always adequate to analyse parenting experiences. I propose to examine parenthood in the context of three types of work that are carried out in connection to it. These are: care work, paid work and domestic work. Even though there are not always clear boundaries between these types of work, their separate analysis enables an understanding of the inequalities in economic status and gender between different parents. Cultural norms about care, gender beliefs, economic and social resources as well as instruments of family policy and labour market requirements create different opportunity structures for different individuals. In this analysis, I assume that parents are reflexive agents who can assess their situation (i.e. their opportunity structures) and during the in-depth interviews can share with others how they experience parenting in the context of the three above mentioned types of work. The narratives of Polish parents pave the way for a critical analysis of inequalities in economic status and gender that prevail in family life and in the labour market in Poland.

# References

Bäck-Wiklund, M., van der Lippe, T., den Dulk, L., & Doorne-Huiskes, A. (Eds.). (2011). *Quality of life and work in Europe: Theory, practice and policy*. Palgrave Macmillan UK. https://doi.org/10.1057/9780230299443.

Bales, R. F., & Parsons, T. (Eds.). (1955). *Family, socialization and interaction process*. Free Press.

Balzarini, R. N., Dharma, C., Kohut, T., Holmes, B. M., Campbell, L., Lehmiller, J. J., et al. (2019). Demographic comparison of American individuals in polyamorous and monogamous relationships. *The Journal of Sex Research, 56*(6), 681–694. https://doi.org/10.1080/00224499.2018.1474333.

Boje, T. P. (2006). Working time and caring strategies: Parenthood in different welfare states. In A. L. Ellingsæter & A. Leira (Eds.), *Politicising parenthood in Scandinavia: Gender relations in welfare states* (pp. 195–215). Policy Press.

Bonstead-Bruns, M. (2007). Work, sociology of. In *The Blackwell encyclopedia of sociology*. John Wiley & Sons. https://doi.org/10.1002/9781405165518.wbeosw025.

Chang, H.-J. (2014). *Economics: The user's guide*. Pelican.

Coltrane, S. (2000). Research on household labor: Modeling and measuring the social embeddedness of routine family work. *Journal of Marriage and Family, 62*(4), 1208–1233. https://doi.org/10.1111/j.1741-3737.2000.01208.x.

Connell, R. (2009). *Gender: In world perspective*. Polity.

Crespi, I., & Ruspini, E. (Eds.). (2016). *Balancing work and family in a changing society: The fathers' perspective*. Palgrave Macmillan.

Doucet, A. (2004). 'It's almost like I have a job, but I don't get paid': Fathers at home reconfiguring work, care, and masculinity. *Fathering: A Journal of Theory, Research, and Practice about Men as Fathers, 2*(3), 277–303. https://doi.org/10.3149/fth.0203.277.

Drobnič, S., & Guillén, A. M. (Eds.). (2011). *Work-life balance in Europe: The role of job quality*. Palgrave Macmillan.

Elias, N. (1978). *What is sociology?* Columbia University Press.

Elias, N. (2000). *The civilizing process* (2nd ed.). Wiley-Blackwell.

Ellingsæter, A. L., & Gulbrandsen, L. (2007). Closing the childcare gap: The interaction of childcare provision and mothers' agency in Norway. *Journal of Social Policy, 36*(4), 649–669. https://doi.org/10.1017/S0047279407001225.
Engels, F. (1884/2010). *The origin of the family, private property, and the state*. Penguin Classics.
Esping-Andersen, G. (1990). *The three worlds of welfare capitalism*. Princeton University Press.
Esping-Andersen, G. (2002). *Why we need a new welfare state*. Oxford University Press.
European Commission. (2013). *Barcelona objectives: The development of childcare facilities for young children in Europe with a view to sustainable and inclusive growth*. European Union.
Flandrin, J. L. (1979). *Families in former times*. CUP Archive.
Giddens, A. (1991). *Modernity and self-identity: Self and society in the late modern age*. Stanford University Press.
Giullari, S., & Lewis, J. (2005). *The adult worker model family, gender equality and care: The search for new policy principles, and the possibilities and problems of a capabilities approach* (Social Policy and Development Programme Paper Number 19). United Nations Research Institute for Social Development.
Giza-Poleszczuk, A. (2005). *Rodzina a system społeczny: Reprodukcja i kooperacja w perspektywie interdyscyplinarnej*. Wydawnictwa Uniwersytetu Warszawskiego.
Gouldner, A. W. (1970). *The coming crisis of western sociology*. Basic Books.
Greenstein, T. N. (2009). National context, family satisfaction, and fairness in the division of household labor. *Journal of Marriage and Family, 71*(4), 1039–1051. https://doi.org/10.1111/j.1741-3737.2009.00651.x.
Gromada, A. (2017). *Rodzina 500+ jako polityka publiczna – Instytut Studiów Zaawansowanych* (Analizy ISZ). Krytyka Polityczna. http://krytykapolityczna.pl/instytut/analiza-isz-anna-gromada-rodzina-500-jako-polityka-publiczna/
Hanisch, C. (2006). *The personal is political*. https://webhome.cs.uvic.ca/~mserra/AttachedFiles/PersonalPolitical.pdf
Hochschild, A., & Machung, A. (2003). *The second shift*. Penguin Books.
Javornik, J., & Kurowska, A. (2017). Work and care opportunities under different parental leave systems: Gender and class inequalities in northern Europe. *Social Policy & Administration, 51*(4), 617–637. https://doi.org/10.1111/spol.12316.
Kimmel, M. S. (2011). *The gendered society* (4th ed.). Oxford University Press.
Kotowska, I. (Ed.). (2014). *Niska dzietność w Polsce w kontekście percepcji Polaków. Diagnoza społeczna 2013 raport tematyczny*. Ministerstwo Pracy i Polityki Społecznej: Centrum Rozwoju Zasobów Ludzkich.
Leitner, S. (2003). Varieties of familialism: The caring function of the family in comparative perspective. *European Societies, 5*(4), 353–375. https://doi.org/10.1080/1461669032000127642.
Lewis, S., Anderson, D., Lyonette, C., Payne, N., & Wood, S. (Eds.). (2017). *Work-life balance in times of recession, austerity and beyond* (1st ed.). Routledge, Taylor & Francis Group.
Marody, M., & Giza-Poleszczuk, A. (2000). Changing images of identity in Poland: From the self-sacrificing to the self-investing woman. In S. Gal & G. Kligman (Eds.), *Reproducing gender: Politics, publics, and everyday life after socialism* (pp. 151–175). Princeton University Press.
Marx, K., & Engels, F. (1848/1969). Manifesto of the communist party. In K. Marx & F. Engels (Eds.), *Karl Marx and Frederick Engels. Selected works: Vol. One* (pp. 98–137). Progress Publishers.
Miller, T. (2005). *Making sense of motherhood: A narrative approach*. Cambridge University Press.
Miller, T. (2011). *Making sense of fatherhood: Gender, caring and work*. Cambridge University Press.
Mizielińska, J. (2017). *Odmienne czy zwyczajne?: Rodziny z wyboru w Polsce*. PWN.
Mizielińska, J., Wasiak-Radoszewski, A., Abramowicz, M., & Stasińska, A. (2014). *Rodziny z wyboru w Polsce życie rodzinne osób nieheteroseksualnych*. Instytut Psychologii Polskiej Akademii Nauk.

# References

Mynarska, M. (2011). Kto planuje mieć dzieci w Polsce do 2015 roku? *Studia Demograficzne, 159* (1), 75–98.
Oakley, A. (2018). *The sociology of housework (reissue).* Policy Press.
Olah, L. S., & Frątczak, E. (Eds.). (2013). *Childbearing, women's employment and work-life balance policies in contemporary Europe.* Palgrave Macmillan.
Orloff, A. (1996). Gender in the welfare state. *Annual Review of Sociology, 22,* 51–78. JSTOR.
Orloff, A. (2009). Gendering the comparative analysis of welfare states: An unfinished agenda. *Sociological Theory, 27*(3), 317–343. https://doi.org/10.1111/j.1467-9558.2009.01350.x.
Parsons, T. (1955). The American family: Its relations to personality and to the social structure. In R. F. Bales & T. Parsons (Eds.), *Family, socialization and interaction process* (pp. 3–34). Free Press.
Paull, G. (2008). Children and women's hours of work. *The Economic Journal, 118*(526), F8–F27. https://doi.org/10.1111/j.1468-0297.2007.02114.x.
Pustułka, P., Struzik, J., & Ślusarczyk, M. (2015). Caught between breadwinning and emotional provisions—The case of Polish migrant fathers in Norway. *Studia Humanistyczne AGH, 14*(2), 117. https://doi.org/10.7494/human.2015.14.2.117.
Reskin, B. F. (2000). Work and occupation. In E. F. Borgatta & R. J. V. Montgomery (Eds.), *Encyclopedia of sociology* (2nd ed.). Macmillan Reference USA.
Ridgeway, C. L., & Correll, S. J. (2004). Unpacking the gender system a theoretical perspective on gender beliefs and social relations. *Gender & Society, 18*(4), 510–531. https://doi.org/10.1177/0891243204265269.
Rogan, F., & Budgeon, S. (2018). The personal is political: Assessing feminist fundamentals in the digital age. *Social Sciences, 7*(8), 132. https://doi.org/10.3390/socsci7080132.
Rowland, D. T. (2007). Historical trends in childlessness. *Journal of Family Issues, 28*(10), 1311–1337. https://doi.org/10.1177/0192513X07303823.
Ruzik-Sierdzińska, A. (2017). *Czy program "Rodzina 500+" wywołał efekt na rynku pracy?* (Analiza No. 15). Instytut Obywatelski.
Saxonberg, S. (2013). From defamilialization to degenderization: Toward a new welfare typology. *Social Policy & Administration, 47*(1), 26–49. https://doi.org/10.1111/j.1467-9515.2012.00836.x.
Saxonberg, S. (2014). *Gendering family policies in post-Communist Europe: A historical-institutional analysis.* Palgrave Macmillan.
Saxonberg, S., Hašková, H., & Mudrák, J. (2012). The development of Czech childcare policies. *SOCIOLOGICKÉ NAKLADATELSTVÍ (SLON).*
Schober, P. S. (2013). The parenthood effect on gender inequality: Explaining the change in paid and domestic work when British couples become parents. *European Sociological Review, 29*(1), 74–85. https://doi.org/10.1093/esr/jcr041.
Sikorska, M. (2019). *Praktyki rodzinne i rodzicielskie we współczesnej Polsce—Rekonstrukcja codzienności.* Wydawnictwo Naukowe Scholar.
Slany, K. (2002). *Alternatywne formy życia małżeńsko-rodzinnego w ponowoczesnym świecie.* Nomos.
Slany, K. (2013). Ponowoczesne rodziny—Konstruowanie więzi i pokrewieństwa. In K. Slany (Ed.), *Zagadnienia małżeństwa i rodzin w perspektywie feministyczno-genderowej.* Wydawnictwo Uniwersytetu Jagiellońskiego.
Ślusarczyk, M. (2019). *Transnarodowe życie rodzin: Na przykładzie polskich migrantów w Norwegii (Wydanie I).* Wydawnictwo Uniwersytetu Jagiellońskiego.
Sobotka, T. (2017). Childlessness in Europe: Reconstructing long-term trends among women born in 1900–1972. In M. Kreyenfeld & D. Konietzka (Eds.), *Childlessness in Europe: Contexts, causes, and consequences* (pp. 17–53). Springer. https://doi.org/10.1007/978-3-319-44667-7_2.
Solera, C., & Mencarini, L. (2018). The gender division of housework after the first child: A comparison among Bulgaria, France and the Netherlands. *Community, Work & Family, 21*(5), 519–540. https://doi.org/10.1080/13668803.2018.1528969.

Spitzmueller, C., & Matthews, R. A. (Eds.). (2016). *Research perspectives on work and the transition to motherhood*. Springer International Publishing.
Standing, G. (2014). *A precariat charter: From denizens to citizens*. Bloomsbury Academic.
Stanisz, A. (2014). *Rodzina made in Poland. Antropologia pokrewieństwa i życia rodzinnego*. Agata Stanisz.
Statistics Poland. (2018). Żłobki i kluby dziecięce w 2017 r.
Suwada, K. (2015). Naturalisation of the difference. The experience of fatherhood in Sweden and Poland. *Studia Humanistyczne AGH, 2*(16), 141–155. https://doi.org/10.7494/human.2015.14.2.141.
Suwada, K. (2017a). *Men, fathering and the gender trap. Sweden and Poland compared*. Palgrave Macmillan.
Suwada, K. (2017b). "It was necessary at the beginning to make this whole revolution": Men's attitudes to parental leaves in Sweden and Poland. *Men and Masculinities, 20*(5), 570–587. https://doi.org/10.1177/1097184X17727571.
Szelewa, D. (2017). From implicit to explicit familialism: Post-1989 family policy reforms in Poland. In *Gender and family in European economic policy* (pp. 129–151). Cham: Palgrave Macmillan.
Szlendak, T. (2011). *Socjologia rodziny: Ewolucja, historia, zróżnicowanie*. Wydawnictwo Naukowe PWN.
Tancred, P. (1995). Women's work: A challenge to the sociology of work. *Gender, Work & Organization, 2*(1), 11–20. https://doi.org/10.1111/j.1468-0432.1995.tb00023.x.
Titkow, A. (2012). Figura Matki Polki. Próba demitologizacji. In E. Korolczuk & R. E. Hryciuk (Eds.), *Pożegnanie z Matką Polką? Dyskursy, praktyki i reprezentacje macierzyństwa we współczesnej Polsce* (pp. 27–47). Wydawnictwo Uniwersytetu Warszawskiego.
Titkow, A., Duch-Krzystoszek, D., & Budrowska, B. (2004). *Nieodpłatna praca kobiet: Mity, realia, perspektywy*. Wydawnictwo IFiS PAN.
Tomescu-Dubrow, I., Dubrow, J. K., Kiersztyn, A., Andrejuk, K., Kolczynska, M., & Slomczynski, K. M. (2019). *The subjective experience of joblessness in Poland*. Springer.
Urbańska, S. (2015). *Matka Polka na odległość: Z doświadczeń migracyjnych robotnic 1989-2010*. Wydawnictwo Naukowe Uniwersytetu Mikołaja Kopernika.
Urbańska, S. (2016). Transnational motherhood and forced migration. Causes and consequences of the migration of Polish working-class women 1989–2010. *Central and Eastern European Migration Review, 5*(1), 109–128.
van der Lippe, T., de Ruijter, J., de Ruijter, E., & Raub, W. (2011). Persistent inequalities in time use between men and women: A detailed look at the influence of economic circumstances, policies, and culture. *European Sociological Review, 27*(2), 164–179. https://doi.org/10.1093/esr/jcp066.
van der Lippe, T., Jager, A., & Kops, Y. (2006). Combination pressure: The paid work: Family balance of men and women in European countries. *Acta Sociologica, 49*(3), 303–319. https://doi.org/10.1177/0001699306067711.
van Eeden-Moorefield, B., & Demo, D. H. (2007). Family diversity. In G. Ritzer (Ed.), *The Blackwell encyclopedia of sociology*. John Wiley & Sons, Ltd. https://doi.org/10.1002/9781405165518.wbeosf012.
Warren, T. (2003). Class and gender-based working time? Time poverty and the division of domestic labour. *Sociology, 37*(4), 733–752. https://doi.org/10.1177/00380385030374006.
West, C., & Fenstermaker, S. (1995). Doing difference. *Gender & Society, 9*(1), 8–38. https://doi.org/10.1177/089124395009001002.
West, C., & Zimmerman, D. H. (1987). Doing gender. *Gender & Society, 1*(2), 125–151. https://doi.org/10.1080/13668803.2012.722008.
West, C., & Zimmerman, D. H. (2009). Accounting for doing gender. *Gender & Society*, 112–122. https://doi.org/10.1177/0891243208326529.
Wrench, J., Rea, A., & Ouali, N. (Eds.). (2016). *Migrants, ethnic minorities and the labour market: Integration and exclusion in Europe*. Springer.

# References

Zachorowska-Mazurkiewicz, A. (2016). *Praca kobiet w teorii ekonomii: Perspektywa ekonomii głównego nurtu i ekonomii feministycznej*. Wydawnictwo Uniwersytetu Jagiellońskiego.

Zachorowska-Mazurkiewicz, A. (2017). Gender, unpaid labour and economics. *Acta Universitatis Lodziensis. Folia Oeconomica, 6*(326), 121–132. https://doi.org/10.18778/0208-6018.326.08.

Zelditch, M. (1955). Role differentiation in the nuclear family: A comparative study. In R. F. Bales & T. Parsons (Eds.), *Family, socialization and interaction process* (pp. 307–353). Free Press.

Żurek, A. (2020). Kobiety a instytucjonalizacja i deinstytucjonalizacja rodziny. *Przegląd Socjologiczny, 69*(1), 9–25. https://doi.org/10.26485/PS/2020/69.1/1.

**Open Access** This chapter is licensed under the terms of the Creative Commons Attribution 4.0 International License (http://creativecommons.org/licenses/by/4.0/), which permits use, sharing, adaptation, distribution and reproduction in any medium or format, as long as you give appropriate credit to the original author(s) and the source, provide a link to the Creative Commons license and indicate if changes were made.

The images or other third party material in this chapter are included in the chapter's Creative Commons license, unless indicated otherwise in a credit line to the material. If material is not included in the chapter's Creative Commons license and your intended use is not permitted by statutory regulation or exceeds the permitted use, you will need to obtain permission directly from the copyright holder.

# Chapter 3
# Care Work and Parenting

**Abstract** This chapter deals with the organisation of care work by Polish parents. Using the data from in-depth interviews and survey data, I demonstrate cultural norms about care that prevails in Polish society. Strong gendered norms and instruments of family policy shape different opportunity structures for men and women. I focus on how parental leaves are used and perceived by Polish parents. I argue that they are still seen primarily as women's right. I analyse the reasoning lying behind such thinking, but also show the experiences of parents who decided to share the leave. Then I proceed to the organisation of care in the context of so-called *care gap*. The Polish system of parental leaves is incompatible with the system of institutional care for children. Consequently, in the period between the end of paid leave and the time when a child can go to a kindergarten parents have to develop different strategies how to provide care for their children. I show how these strategies differ in the context of economic inequalities, as well as what consequences care gap has on gender inequalities. Finally, the chapter finishes with the analysis of how care work is perceived by parents.

**Keywords** Care work · Parenting · Gender roles · Gender inequalities · Poland · Family policy

## 3.1 Culture of Care in Poland

This chapter is about a particular type of work that is strictly connected to parenthood—caregiving, 'the physical, engaged and embodied work of caring for children' (Ranson 2015, p. 1). As Julia Kubisa notes, care is one of the oldest relationships that is important for people through their whole lives (Kubisa 2014, p. 79). Care work is fundamental for the functioning of society, therefore as I'm analysing the experiences of parenting in Polish society I'm starting with the experiences connected with care work. The organisation of care work is strictly connected with norms and values prevailing in a particular society. These norms and values specify the acceptable forms of providing and receiving care. In contemporary times, we can distinguish two main agents of care provision—family and the welfare state. Family is a social institution which is primarily responsible for providing care for its members. The main role of the welfare state is to support family. This role started to be recognised in the twentieth century as the welfare state developed. In this context 'care as work includes formal/informal as well as private/public significations' (Pfau-Effinger and Rostgaard 2011, p. 2). The following analysis of caregiving in the context of parenting takes into consideration both the engagement of family (in particular parents), as well as the support of the Polish welfare state in providing care for children. In this book, I concentrate mostly on children under school age, since in their case care is the most demanding work requiring day-to-day, intensive involvement.

The support of the Polish welfare state is strictly connected with the culture of care prevailing in Polish society. I take 'the culture of care' here to mean socially acceptable patterns of care practices that serve as important guides for people in their everyday behaviours (Pfau-Effinger and Rostgaard 2011). In the context of caring for children, the most important norms are those which impose obligations on family members, in particular women. Data from the International Social Survey Programme (ISSP) in 2012 clearly shows that in Polish society more than 75% of people thought that family members should be the primary care givers for children under school age. Only 14% thought it should be government agencies. Men (81%) more often than women (75%) indicate family members, yet even among women the numbers are still very high (see Graph 3.1).

But it must be noted that not every family member is responsible to the same extent when it comes to providing care for their children. The ISSP data clearly shows that there are different expectations towards mothers and fathers. In the survey there were two questions about the organisation of family life and work life in families with a child under school age. Most people agreed that the best way of organising life is when a father works full-time, whereas a mother is at home or works part-time. Yet what is particularly interesting is that over 40% of people think that the worst option is when a father is at home and the mother works full-time. For these people such a situation is worse than one in which both parents work full-time (see Graphs 3.2 and 3.3). This data clearly shows that the provision of childcare is not perceived as a man's main obligation—it is women who are expected to take a break from paid work or at least reduce working hours when they have children.

These norms are reinforced by the Polish family policy system, which is explicitly genderising and does not recognise fathers as potential caregivers. Thus when looking at the organisation of care work in Polish families it is important to look at gender inequalities and analyse how gender is done in connection to parenthood. As I underlined in the previous chapter, care work is perceived as a woman's duty. Men's engagement in caregiving is often seen in terms of help or support. Such societal convictions determine differences in experiencing parenthood by men and women. What interests me here is the micro perspective—the perspective of individuals who have to struggle with cultural norms about childcare that are often in conflict with the requirements of the labour market and obligations resulting from paid work. I adopt here the theoretical perspective of agency to see how individuals act in particular social settings, how they function in *opportunity structures* resulting

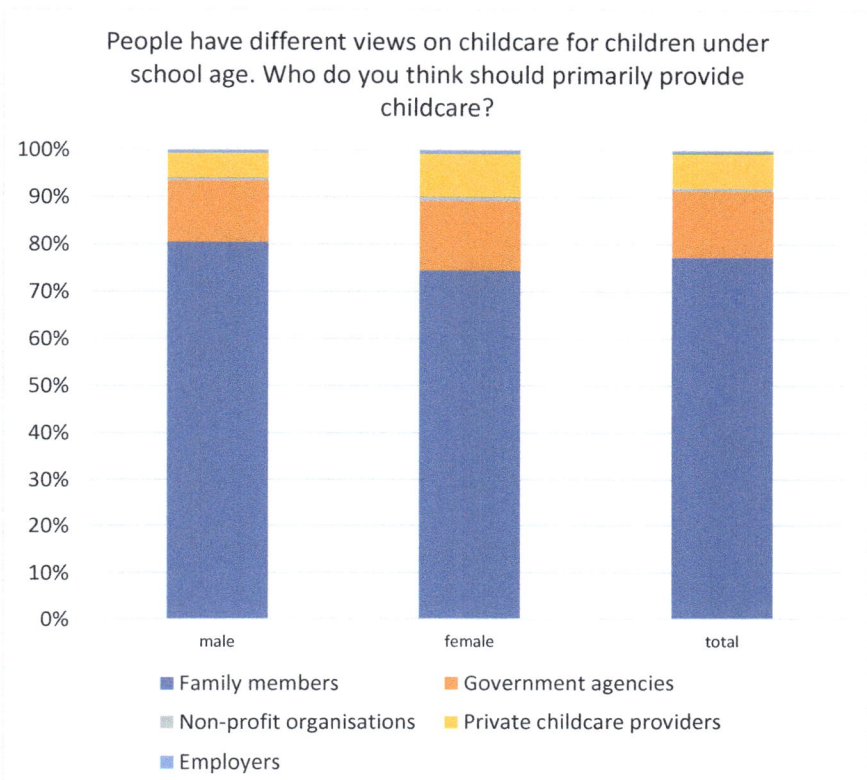

**Graph 3.1** Provision of childcare. Source ISSP 2012. Prepared by the author

from the family policy system, as well as cultural norms and values. In this chapter, I am particularly interested in how these opportunity structures affect everyday practices and decisions about the organisation of childcare. The two main instruments aimed at supporting parents in providing care are parental leave and institutional care in nurseries and kindergartens, thus in the following sections I first analyse how parents use leave and then proceed to the organisation of care work after the periods of paid leave.

## 3.2 "I Can't Imagine My Husband on Parental Leave". Parental Leave as a Mother's Right

Most of the interviewed parents had a right to 52 weeks of maternity and parental leave. All interviewed fathers had a right to two weeks of paternity leave. As I underlined in the previous chapter, the Polish parental leave system is explicitly

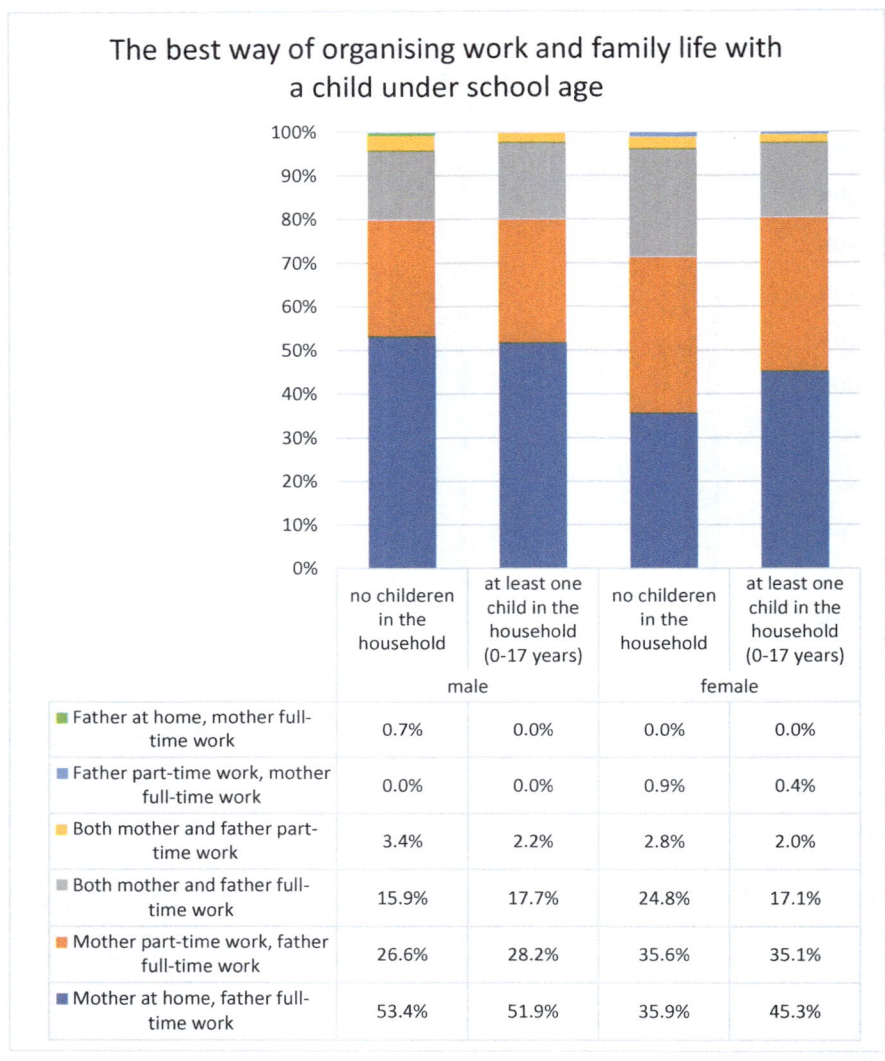

**Graph 3.2** Consider a family with a child under school age. What, in your opinion, is the best way for them to organise their work and family life? Source ISSP 2012. Prepared by the author

genderising. Even though in 2013 the new type of leave was introduced—parental leave—as a right of both parents, men are not encouraged to actually use it. Mothers are still its main recipients. The data from the Social Insurance Institutions shows that men are only 1% of the recipients of parental leave allowance (in 2017 only 4200 men received the allowance in comparison to 402,400 women). Fathers more often take two weeks of paternity leave, which is not transferable to the mother—in 2017 there were 174,000 men who took this leave, the number significantly

3.2 "I Can't Imagine My Husband on Parental Leave". Parental Leave as a Mother's... 37

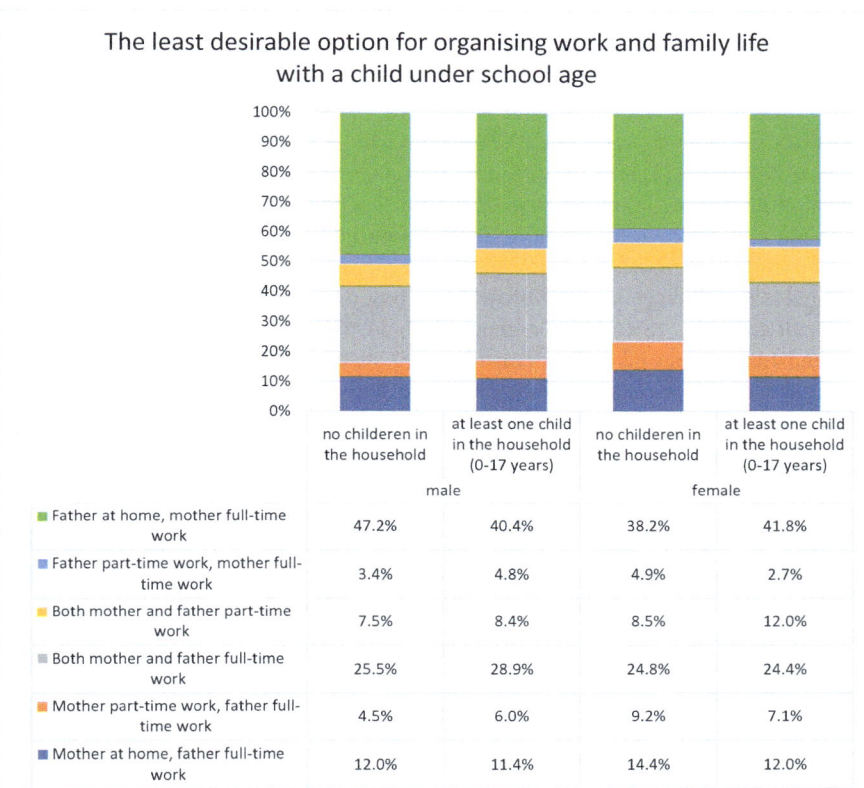

**Graph 3.3** Consider a family with a child under school age. What, in your opinion, is the least desirable way for them to organise their work and family life? Source ISSP 2012. Prepared by the author

increased from 2013 when only 28,600 men took paternity leave.[1] Yet since this leave is usually taken when mothers are on maternity leave directly after the child's birth or during the summer holidays, these numbers do not say much about men's engagement in caregiving. Thus in the following analysis I concentrate on parents' attitudes to parental leave, on how the leave was used, whether it was shared or not, and also what interviewees thought about the idea of forcing/encouraging men to take longer periods of such leave. Parents' thoughts and beliefs show how care work is perceived in the context of gender inequalities. They are also a good illustration of gender beliefs prevailing in Polish society.

Jana Javornik and Anna Kurowska (2017) analysed parental leave as an instrument that 'shape[s] individuals' real opportunities to be and do around the family's

---

[1] Data from the database of the Social Insurance Institution in Poland, available at: https://www.zus.pl/baza-wiedzy/statystyka (access 11-03-2020).

first critical turning point – the arrival of a child' (2017, p. 618). Parental leave creates three types of opportunity structure: 'opportunity to stay in the labour market while having a child; to care personally for a child; a child's opportunity to be cared for by both parents' (Javornik and Kurowska 2017, p. 622). The most important aspect of their analysis is socio-economic and gender inequalities in opportunities—the parental leave system of different European countries creates different *real* opportunities for men and women, as well as for individuals with different socio-economic situations. What is more, real opportunities do not necessarily turn into actual practices, as individuals do not always take advantage of their opportunities. The analysis of Javornik and Kurowska is based on quantitative data from eight European countries (Sweden, Denmark, Iceland, Estonia, Norway, Lithuania, Finland and Latvia) and takes into consideration such criteria as the legal equality of men and women on paper, non-transferable leave, income replacement rate and congruency of leave with public childcare. In my analysis I focus only on one country—Poland—and examine the opportunity structures of parents using qualitative data from in-depth interviews with mothers and fathers. Referring to the theoretical perspective of agency, I assume that individuals possess *reflexivity*, which allows them to assess social conditions and consequently their real opportunities and so make decisions about how they take advantage of them (Caetano 2015). This means that parents can evaluate the parental leave system and use the leave according to their own preferences.

The interviews clearly indicate the lack of equality between mothers and fathers in taking the opportunity to care personally for a child, as well as to stay in the labour market when becoming a parent. In most cases, the interviewed women used every week of maternity and parental leave, whereas men used only two weeks of paternity leave. Such a situation is taken for granted by most parents and not questioned. The interviewed men generally did not take parental leave because of economic and/or 'biological' reasons.

The economic reasons were strictly connected with paid work. Men still earn more than women in Poland, taking parental leave means getting benefit on the level of 80% of salary (or in some cases 60%). For many families it means losing more money when a father is on parental leave. In the case of self-employed men, the loss is even greater, since they receive the benefit on the level of 80% of the minimum wage. Additionally, many interviewed parents openly admit that a father cannot stop working for a longer period than two weeks. Most men, regardless of their working position, have a great sense of duty towards their paid work, co-workers or/and employers.

> R: And your husband cannot go on leave, since he is self-employed. Is it right?
> I: In theory, he could, because ZUS[2] is paying, but it's the level of minimum wage, so it would have huge consequences for our earnings. Because 80% of wage is still ok, but now

---

[2]The abbreviation of Zakład Ubezpieczeń Społecznych, which is the Social Insurance Institution in Poland.

## 3.2 'I Can''t Imagine My Husband on Parental Leave'. Parental Leave as a Mother''s... 39

> [the husband] is earning three times more than me, so it is a big difference for us. [C6W8 Ida][3]

> R: Did you ever consider taking parental leave?
> I: In fact, it wouldn't change much for me. I mean, I'd still have the same responsibilities, because of the type of work I do with all its related obligations, so it didn't make sense for me. [S8 M17 Zbigniew, manager in a small enterprise]

The second quote is a perfect illustration of men's attitudes to parental leave for men. Many men, regardless of their situation in the labour market, prioritise paid work. Going on leave would mean that they would still be fulfilling duties resulting from paid work. This prioritisation applies to men in different positions (skilled and unskilled employees), with different salaries and different types of employment. From an economic perspective, the opportunity structures of fathers with higher salaries are even more limited, since they lose more money on parental leave than men with a lower income. Yet the data from the interviews indicates that regardless of their level of income men are not willing to actually take the leave.

The economic reasoning is reinforced by thinking in terms of biological differences between men and women. The most common argument against sharing parental leave was breastfeeding (see also: Reimann 2016). The interviewed mothers, especially, emphasised that in their case sharing leave with their partner would mean the interruption of breastfeeding. They often felt that it would be emotionally too difficult to go back to work and leave a child with the father.

> I don't know if I was ready for this [sharing the leave] either. My son was so incredibly small. I was breastfeeding him until he was, I'd say, over a year and a half. There were also various different psychological conditions in play too. [C3W4 Joanna]

> R: Did you consider an option in which your husband takes part of the parental leave?
> I: I mean, I must admit that I can't imagine breastfeeding while my husband would be on leave. I also wanted to breastfeed at least one year, so it was impossible, wasn't it? Well, it couldn't be done. I used the breast pump a lot, because I had these classes, I had to go to them. So once a week, when I went there, there were three bottles prepared for my son and I was away for six hours, so [my husband] fed him every two hours. [C4W5 Ela]

The biological differences between mothers and fathers in using parental leave are clearly underlined here, even by these parents who have a rather equalitarian approach to the division of domestic and care work as well as involvement in paid work. Breastfeeding is used as an indisputable argument, even though many Polish mothers have serious problems with it—a report from 2018 shows that only 41% of women exclusively breastfeed their new-born child, 10% is feeding with baby formula and the rest is combining breastfeeding with other forms of feeding. Only 28.83% of mothers plan to exclusively breastfeed until the child is one year old, and 16.66% until the child is two years old (Iwanowicz-Palus and Bogusz 2018). The

---

[3]Abbreviations mean: C—coupled parent, S—single parent, W—woman, M—man. All names of interviewees have been changed, whereas names mentioned in the interviews were removed to reassure confidentiality. Similarly, all information and facts that might help identify interviewees were also modified or removed.

World Health Organisation recommends exclusive breastfeeding for the first six months. which means that sharing leave should not necessarily be an obstacle to breastfeeding, since fathers usually take leave when a child is over six months (O'Brien and Wall 2017). As I argue in my other analysis of fatherhood (Suwada 2015, 2017a), using biology is one of the strategies to legitimise prevailing gender inequalities. In the process of *naturalisation* the initial biological differences between men and women serve as an explanation for gender inequalities in the household and other social spheres. The same process applies here, even though many couples did not consider sharing parental leave at all but considered it by default to be a mother's right, when asked about the reasons they referred to biological explanations. Analysis of the interviews indicates that many parents were not actually aware of how the parental leave system is constructed in Poland. As was mentioned in the previous chapter, the system went through some significant reforms during the previous years, and only recently were men included as recipients of parental leave, but it can be assumed that expectant parents would check what rights they have to assess their opportunity structures. It is clear that they just check the length of the leave for a mother and the replacement rate. What might be even more surprising is that the lack of awareness that parental leave is also a father's right applies mostly to men. A few of the researched fathers learned during the interview that they had a right to use some part of the parental leave.

> R: Let's proceed to the issue of parental leave. Your wife had used maternity and parental leave...
> I: Parental leave? What's that?
> R: There was six months of maternity leave and then six months of parental leave.
> I: Oh ... she was at home for one year, I thought it was all maternity leave. [C4M5 Aleksander]

In this context, it is clear that the *real* opportunity structures of mothers and fathers are not the same. A woman's opportunity to stay in the labour market while having a child is limited by economic conditions, as well as gender beliefs grounded in naturalised thinking about the different roles of mothers and fathers. Similarly, a man's opportunity to care personally for a child or a child's opportunity to be cared for by two parents are also constrained by the same factors. This means that it is not enough to provide legal opportunity structures, but there is also a need to introduce more incentives for fathers to use that leave even if it would undermine prevailing gender beliefs about parenting.

In this context, it is interesting to look at the situation of parents who shared their parental leave. This is not a common situation in Polish society. In the samples there were six couples who shared their leave, so we cannot draw any generalisations based on their experiences, but they can serve as a lens through which it is possible to observe the consequences of breaking cultural gender norms about care. In the case of four of the couples, the father took at least two months of parental leave. In the two others the father took a different type of leave to be with a small child (four

## 3.2 "I Can't Imagine My Husband on Parental Leave". Parental Leave as a Mother's...

months of unpaid, extended leave and a one-year-long health improvement leave[4]). All of these couples were middle class, with higher education and both parents worked, their salaries were similar, but in a few cases the women earned more. All of them lived in big cities. What is more, all of them had a very equalitarian approach and were very aware of existing gender inequalities.

The most common motivation for fathers to go on leave was responsibility for their child and a sense of fairness for their partner, less often economic reasons or the need to fill a care gap resulting from the fact that the mother needed to return to her paid work but there were no available places in childcare institutions.

> So I think that if there is a possibility, and we have here such a possibility, then it is simply an issue of basic logic and decency that both men and women should take parental leave for the same period of time. [C7M8 Stefan]

> I mean, I understand that this is still sort of ... pretty rare, but ... but I don't see why. In a sense this is definitely the most important event in my life ... the birth of [my son] and ... um ... I mean, I understand that sometimes the financial situation is what it is, and that [couples have] such agreements and ... um ... and that you can't, you simply can't [take leave as a father]. Er ... but there are also people who don't even take these two weeks off ... right after the birth. And for me this is ... this is just f*****g ... it's just ... totally irresponsible I guess, I don't know. [C11M12 Arek]

Contrary to other parents, those who shared leave very carefully assessed their opportunity structures and divided the leave in the most convenient way. They took into consideration the economic dimension and the paid work situation of both the mother and the father as well as the issue of their children's well-being. In the context of everyday practices, the father's time on parental leave has the most significant consequences for changes in relationship dynamics in the family. As a mother stays at home, she is the most important parent for children. The shift of the main caregiver results in a better relationship between a father and a child, and as such undermines the prevailing gender beliefs and norms about care. A mother often stops being regarded as the only one who can solve problems or give comfort in a difficult situation.

> So it was a time when the relationship with my child was changing all the time, because it was when she was six months till twelve months, and this is a period when a child is changing from day to day and you cannot get used to anything. So my relationship with her was changing every day. But I also think I had a better relationship with her after these six months too, because she didn't only see me when I returned tired from work. [C7M8 Stefan]

> It was a very nice time to ... know my son, you know? Because during the ten months my wife was on leave, for me nothing had changed. I went to work at 8 a.m., was back at 5.30 and I did not have much time left. One hour or one and half hours of playing, supper, washing and getting him to sleep [...]. So for these two months it was a great idea to get to know each other and also to learn how to spend time with a kid. [C6M7 Krzysztof]

---

[4]This type of leave is available for teachers after seven years of work. In this case the leave was taken to improve health, but also to fill the care gap after paid parental leave (more on the care gap later in this chapter).

The situation of men on parental leave also frequently improves the relationship between partners, because fathers started to recognise that care work is a difficult task that can be troublesome and boring. This period also helps to better organise the division of domestic work when parental leave ends and both parents need to return to work. None of the couples regretted that they shared parental leave, but this does not mean that the situation of reversing traditional gender roles was *normal* for the rest of society. The reactions of other people indicate that care work is not perceived as work done by men. Even though most parents received a rather positive reaction from other people, it was sometimes met with shock and consternation.

> R: How did your colleagues react to your leave?
> I: Oh, well ... one colleague who couldn't wait to get back to work [after two weeks of paternity leave] was a little bit surprised, because for him it was different. He was happy to leave his wife at home with their son [laugh]. He sat in an air-conditioned office for 9-10 hours a day, so he could be back home later. [C6M7 Krzysztof]

Other people openly expressed their admiration for men taking parental leave.

> Basically, all my male colleagues and friends told me something I didn't understand at all. They'd say, "Stefan, I admire you" or "aren't you afraid?" and so on. I didn't understand it at all. These questions simply blew my mind, and when I heard them, I started to laugh. I mean, I don't know, what is there to admire? It was a wonderful time which I spent with my child. [P7M8 Stefan]

Such a situation is particularly difficult for mothers who have a greater sense of injustice. On the one hand, they are not admired for taking parental leave, it is expected of them, but nobody treats them as a heroine when they do it. On the other hand, they also feel the pressure that they need to be with their children as long as possible, sharing leave means they spend less time with their children, and consequently may be branded 'a bad mother'.

> I had such a moment two weeks before I was supposed to return to paid work, I had a crisis, our son had separation fears and additionally everyone was telling me: "What are you doing? He needs a mother, you're still breastfeeding him. How is this supposed to work? It can't work." I was also questioning myself as a mother, thinking that I should stay with him. [C11W13 Sylwia]

> Yes, you know, it just pisses me off that people are saying things [to my partner] like "I admire you" or "how are you handling that?" or something like that. Nobody is telling me that they admire me for taking six months of maternity leave. [...] And I was so angry at my mum, because she asked if [my partner] would be ok at work because of taking leave ... And I was so angry because I had a short-term contract, my boss was super weird, so looking objectively I might have had bigger problems with this situation. [C7W9 Stefa]

Such reactions clearly show that Polish society puts strong pressure on women to be the main caregiver in a couple, and does not recognise fathers as caregivers . As Nancy Dowd notes 'fathers are treated as volunteers, while mothers are draftees' (Dowd 2000, p. 7). Men can choose to what extent they engage in care practices, whereas women do not have a choice—they have to be engaged and they are *lucky* if their male partner chooses the path of involved fatherhood (Hanlon 2012; Miller 2011).

During the interviews all parents were also asked what they thought about the idea of introducing four months of parental leave reserved for fathers.[5] So the situation of the interview gave parents the opportunity to reflect on men's right to parental leave, even if they did not consider it for themselves. This also gave them an opportunity to reflect on the gendered nature of care work. The idea arouses mixed feelings. On the one hand, there were people who were against it. They most often referred to biological differences between men and women, and the fact that it is not appropriate to force people (in this case fathers) to do something that they do not want to do. Fathers should have a choice if they want to take parental leave, and parents as a couple should have a right to choose how they divide periods of leave between themselves. At the same time only one interviewed mother said that in her opinion it was unfair that there are 14 weeks of obligatory maternity leave for every mother. The right to choose is thus defended only in the case of men.

> No, this [parental leave for fathers] is already way too compulsory, and it's forcing men and women to have equal rights, mixing their rolls [sic], roles, which are not the same because men and women have completely different biological roles. So no, I don't agree with such egalitarianism where women are forced to give up some of their privileges because this is thought to be bothersome, and that this man ought to have these, these privileges. [C5M6 Filip]

> I don't know, I'm not sure. If it [non-transferable leave for fathers] was, then everybody would use it, I'm sure about it. But would this father really help a mother with a little baby? You know, a little baby really needs such a superdad when they are one and a half years old, maybe two years old, then a dad can show them the world, but a mum is . . . no matter how a dad is trying, a mum is always more important, isn't she? [S11W28 Urszula]

On the other hand, there are parents who did not share parental leave, but they still think it is a good idea. They recognised the double burden which women have, and the need for the greater engagement of men in domestic and care work. Some mothers also noted that this might be a way of making men aware that taking care of children and the household is hard work that needs to be more appreciated.

> I support this. I couldn't support it more. This doesn't mean that I'm a militant feminist, but in this patriarchal world in which we live, such a kick in the ass for all men, who think that staying at home is easy, simple and nice and that children need mostly women, is needed. Then it might turn out that fathers can take this leave, because now either employers are not happy or daddies are saying "it'd be easier for you [to take this leave]". But if those four months [of leave] were either taken by the father or lost, then it would be a different story. I'm sure of it. [C13W17 Magdalena]

> I think this is not a bad idea, because it forces men to, for example, take over some of the duties from women . . . and if he takes care of the child, then he gains some kind of know-how. You need to know how to change a nappy or, I don't know, how to dress your child. And if you do it every day, then you know it [. . .]. Because later you want to help, but you have no idea how to do it. [C1M1 Jakub]

---

[5]At that time there was a discussion in the European Commission on introducing four months of parental leave reserved for a father in all EU member states.

These intuitions of interviewed parents are to some extent confirmed by other research on care work and fatherhood. Men's engagement in care work helps them understand that it is hard work, and consequently they appreciate the work done by their female partners in connection to parenthood. What is more, engagement in care work can help to change men's attitudes to gender beliefs and prevailing gender roles, as well as notice the cultural dimension of masculinity and femininity models (Brandth and Kvande 2016; Elliott 2016; Hanlon 2012; Ranson 2015; Scambor et al. 2014).

## 3.3 "Nurseries Are So Expensive...". The Care Gap and Organisation of Care After Parental Leave

The period of parental leave, although based on traditional gender roles, is a relatively unproblematic time for parents. For one year they have a right to highly paid parental leave, and one parent, usually the mother, can temporarily leave her paid work without greater economic loss or other complications. The problem arises with the end of paid leave. The Polish family system is characterised by a lack of congruency between the parental leave system and the system of institutional care for children. This means that when paid parental leave ends there is a problem of finding a place for a one-year-old child in a nursery. As written in Chap. 2 institutional care for children in Poland is a two-tier system, in which there are two types of institutions—nurseries for children under three and preschools for children aged 3–6 years. In 2017 only 8.6% of children under three were enrolled in a nursery, which means that there is a huge demand for the care of the youngest children. This lack of congruency between the parental leave system and institutional care for children under three I call here *the care gap* (see: Farstad 2015; Ingólfsdóttir and Gíslason 2016; Suwada 2020). The care gap creates a serious organisational challenge for parents in Poland. It generates structural inequalities between parents and limits their opportunity structures in organising care for their children. In the following analysis, I depict the main strategies that interviewed parents adopt to deal with the care gap. What interests me here is how economic and gender inequalities affect opportunity structures of different parents. The structural conditions generated by the welfare state, as well as gender beliefs about care and labour market requirements, creates distinctly different possibilities for mothers and fathers, as well as for people with different economic resources and in different labour market situations. Cultural norms around care put more pressure on women to deal with the problem of the care gap, whereas economic resources allow richer parents to *buy* care on the free market.

The interviews indicate that the period between the end of paid parental leave and the beginning of preschool when a child is three years old is the most problematic for parents when it comes to the organisation of care work. This is because of the previously mentioned care gap and the lack of places in childcare institutions for children under three, but these dilemmas are also reinforced by cultural norms about care. In particular the myth of threeness (see Chap. 2) intensifies the pressure put on women to take a break from work in connection with motherhood. Based on analysis of the interviews here are the four most common strategies for organising care: (1) sending a child to a nursery (usually a private one), (2) hiring a baby-sitter, (3) getting help from a grandmother (less often a grandfather) and (4) women withdrawing from paid work. The choice between these strategies is usually connected with the socio-economic situation of a family, which either limits or broadens parents', in particular mothers', opportunity structures.

The broadest, although still rather limited, opportunity structures are characteristic for dual breadwinner parents with an average or above average financial situation. Even though they usually cannot afford for one parent to take a break from paid work, they have more options from which they can choose. The most common choice is between nursery (usually a private one) and a baby-sitter. The final decision is a result of economic calculations as well as individual preferences regarding the organisation of care. There are two types of parents—those who decided to send a child to a nursery or those who hired a baby-sitter. Yet the reasoning behind these two choices is very similar. In both cases parents explained their choices referring to social control and the child's safety. In the case of sending a child to a nursery, parents believed that institutions guarantee greater safety since there are many child-care workers, as well as there being other parents, who can notice any unacceptable behaviour.

> To be honest I'd be more afraid of nannies, if I didn't have anyone recommended, than a nursery. Because in a nursery you have this social control, there are more carers, there are a lot of parents. If something bad happens, then it will be recognised sooner. [C1W1 Jola]

Whereas according to parents who decided to hire a baby-sitter, there is no social control in nurseries. They believe it is better to have a baby-sitter who can come to the child's home and is totally focused on one child. Additionally, it is possible to record what is going on at home (although parents never admitted that they actually did it, they rather mentioned that they knew other people who recorded baby-sitters).

> Before the kindergarten we had a baby-sitter who took care of him. We did not decide on a nursery, because I was not sure about this institution. Mostly because a child who cannot speak ... I have a feeling that such collective care of children who cannot speak and cannot communicate clearly is not the best choice. Fortunately, we can afford to hire a nanny, so when he was one year old, such a lady started to come here. [C6W8 Ida]

What is more, nurseries are problematic for many parents, since children are getting sick more often, especially at the beginning when they start to attend. Consequently, there are parents who withdraw their children from a nursery after one or two months, because their child was sick all the time, and someone needed to stay home with them anyway. Such circumstances clearly show that the economic situation of a family is a crucial determinant of what parents can do. More affluent parents usually find a nanny. In the case of less affluent parents, care work is usually undertaken by grandmothers, who are somehow forced by external conditions to help.

The nursery episode was very short, it only lasted about a month and a half, then that was it. My mother said no, no more nursery, she would not allow the child to waste away [in the nursery], because my daughter she got seriously sick, after starting at the nursery she got double pneumonia, her first serious illness. Then she [the grandmother] took care of her [the granddaughter] for more than a year before she started kindergarten. [S4W6 Iwona]

Children getting sick in nurseries is the most common disincentive that is articulated by parents in the interviews. Yet it is reinforced by the myth of threeness. Many parents openly express negative attitudes to institutional care for children under three. Nurseries are seen as a source of diseases, but also according to some parents, nurseries are not providing enough attention and emotional support for a small child who has been separated from its parents. Consequently, parents are criticised who send their children to a nursery. Such criticism has negative effects, especially on mothers, who feel that they are not fulfilling their role properly. The following exchange clearly represents the problems faced by parents in connection with closing the care gap.

I: As we were saying we were looking for a nursery, that's when we encountered such [...] [my husband] heard that "No, it's better when a child is at home till three with a mum." I also heard such opinions, also from my parents, from my mum, "Sylwia, no, this nursery isn't a good idea". This was a moment when I was really stressed out.
R: Did you consider another option?
I: No, not really [...]. In reality we did not have a choice. In a sense, it was very difficult for us. I am the one who earns more, so if someone was to take a break from work, it was [my husband]. But truly we could not afford it, so we did not consider it. At some point, we thought that maybe [my husband's] mother, who did not work and who had been caring for her other grandchildren till they were three, could help us [...]. But she did not agree. [C11W12 Sylwia]

The societal expectations resulting from gender beliefs and care norms evidently limit parents' opportunity structures and reinforce gender inequalities between mothers and fathers. Yet the economic dimension cannot be ignored here. The interviews with high-income parents show that they do not experience serious problems due to the care gap. The decision whether to send a child to a nursery, hire a nanny or even take a break from paid work for a couple of months resulted from other factors than access to care. Financial resources distinctly broadened opportunity structures for such parents (in particular mothers).

I: With my first daughter I wanted to get back to work fast, so just after maternity leave I went back. I used maternity leave and I wanted to be back at work.
R: Who was taking care of your child?
I: A baby-sitter. We manged to find a good baby-sitter, later she took care of our twin boys. But with the twins it was different [...]. I was also on maternity leave, then I took my holidays and then I took this extended leave, because we were building a house when I was pregnant with the boys. We wanted to move fast, so I used maternity leave and extended leave to decorate the house and move in. [S2K2 Ewa]

Ewa's situation is a good illustration of broad opportunity structures for parents with high economic resources. The decision on the organisation of care was not conditioned by institutional possibilities. Ewa did not refer to any cultural norms about care. Her decisions resulted from her actual needs. Yet it is worth mentioning the gendered character of care—regardless of financial situation it is the woman who is primarily responsible for care. The dilemmas of when to return to work are hardly ever characteristic for men.

Economic resources are a crucial factor that affect the organisation of care in a family and women's opportunity structures. On the one hand, many families cannot afford to live only on one wage and many (especially highly skilled) women do not want to take a break from paid work. There are also many women who have no choice, and are forced to leave the labour market in connection with motherhood. This mostly applies to families with lower economic resources and unskilled workers with low earnings. In the narrative of parents with an average or above average economic situation, the problem of finding a place in a nursery was hardly ever mentioned. This is because these parents could afford to pay for a private nursery which still cost less than the mother could earn. In the case of mothers with low earnings, private nurseries were often financially unattainable, whereas public ones had no places or were not available nearby. What is more, in the case of mothers with lower cultural capital, the question about organisation of care work did not result in descriptions about possible choices, but rather short answers like "I'm not working now" or "I quit". A good example is Pola, who was questioned multiple times on this point by the researcher, so her situation was clearly understood.

> R: When you got pregnant, were you working?
> I: No, I quit.
> R: You quit? Immediately?
> I: No, I went on sick leave ... and then as all leaves were over, I quit.
> R: Why did you quit?
> I: Because there was no one who could take care of my daughter.
> R: Was your husband away?
> I: Yeah, my husband was away and my mum was working.
> R: Didn't you consider any help like a baby-sitter or a nursery?
> I: No, I'm not so mean as to send my child to a nursery. [C12W15 Pola]

Pola's opportunity structures were very limited, because of her care norms she did not even think of using an institutional care system. She was unable to get help from a grandmother who was still active in the labour market. The experiences of low-income parents show that grandparents' help is the only way they can organise care of their children after the period of paid leave. Yet the recent introduction of Family 500+ benefit broadened opportunity structures for some women. Iza is a mother of two children, two and five years old, she lives in a small town and does manual labour in a warehouse. With her first child she returned to work very quickly after half a year of paid maternity leave when her mother-in-law and brother-in-law took care of her son. By the time she had her second child her situation was much improved. In the meantime, paid parental leave and Family 500+ benefit were introduced.

> R: Did your situation improve with the Family 500+ programme?
> I1: Yeah, it did ... I didn't go back to work because at work I would earn less than 1,200 PLN, and now I have three benefits: 500+ for two children plus benefit because of extended parental leave and family benefit. So together I have 1,600 PLN.

I2 (husband's interruption[6]): This is basically your salary.
I1: Yeah, it is.
I2: It's as if you were working ...
I1: Working, yeah. As I was saying, I earned less than 1,300 PLN, so it wasn't worth going back to work if I can get the same money from the state. Because we have so low income that I knew I'd get money, right? So I preferred to stay home with them [the children] rather than going back to work.
R: Because then you would need to find a nursery or something else?
I1: Nursery, yeah. Or mother-in-law, she is retired. There's a nursery in the next town, but it's not so easy getting there. No, to get a place there ... it's a long list, it isn't worth taking ... [C9W11 Iza]

Because Iza did not return to work, they could get the Family 500+ benefit for the first child, but she was eligible for other benefits for low income families. She got more than she could earn and at the same time she did not have to spend money on a nursery or a baby-sitter. Taking into consideration that she performed manual labour in another town where commuting was time consuming, continuing paid work was beneficial neither in economic terms nor in terms of time and emotional costs. Iza claimed that she did not want to completely withdraw from paid work, but planned to find a new job nearer to home when her younger son went to preschool. In such a way the Family 500+ programme broadened her opportunity structures, giving her a chance to close the care gap resulting from institutional settings. In the case of low-income families, the strategy to employ a baby-sitter to take care of children was not mentioned in the interviews at all. It can be assumed that paid work for unskilled women is not a source of satisfaction or self-realisation, and if all the money earned has to be spent on care, paid work does not make any sense.

Keeping in mind the strong gender norm about care for small children, it must be noted that there is no similar reluctance to kindergartens, which are rather treated as educational institutions than care institutions. Almost all interviewed parents sent or planned to send their children to kindergarten when they were over three. These plans were justified by the fact that in kindergarten children learn how to function with other people, they are better socialised and that their bond with parents is not so strong anymore. This suggests that the myth of threeness is still very strong in Poland. Its strength might be connected with the fact that it is congruent with institutional settings, according to which kindergartens are educational institutions and therefore are manged by the Ministry of National Education. At the same time, the educational aspect of nurseries is ignored. They are treated as childcare institutions and are operated by the Ministry of Family, Labour and Social Policy, which is responsible for family policy in Poland.

---

[6]The family lived in one-room flat, so it was impossible to conduct interviews with parents separately. Thus interviews with this couple were often interrupted by the other parent.

## 3.4 "I'm a Bit Down…". Loneliness and Exhaustion in Care Work

I previously focused on the organisation of care during the period of parental leave and the care gap, yet care work is a parents' everyday experience, regardless of whether they use the care services of nurseries, get help from baby-sitters, grandparents or other family members. So I shall now focus on the actual practice of care. I will particularly concentrate on the hardship of care work. As Gillian Ranson observed (2015) involvement in caregiving helps people to recognise its value. This is a crucial aspect of care experiences in contemporary times. Care is undervalued and not recognised as work, which has consequences for prevailing gender inequalities (see also: Elliott 2016; Hanlon 2012; Scambor et al. 2014). Focusing on the hardship of care work helps us to acknowledge its social value and the need to rethink how as a society we perceive people, especially women, who take a break from paid employment on account of care obligations.

Analysis of the interviews shows that caregiving experiences are located between two ends of a continuum. Sometimes caregiving is perceived as a great experience and a precious time to be enjoyed with a child. At other times, caregiving is perceived as being troublesome and laborious. In the interviews, the second type of experience is much more commonly expressed. Therefore, I begin with a description of the difficulties of caregiving before proceeding to the more positive aspects as described. My aim here is also to address the question of what lies behind these different perceptions of care work.

The biggest burden of caring for a small child is that of loneliness and social isolation. When describing their experience of staying at home parents often emphasised that the biggest problem was the lack of conversation with adults. A child is of course a human being, but parents cannot have meaningful and stimulating conversations with them. The lack of contact with other adults is what makes time spent at home with a child distinctly different from time spent at paid work. Some parents, especially mothers, try to organise their everyday life so as to meet with other mothers during the day, yet because of the different schedules children have this often proves extremely difficult.

> For example, during my first parental leave I sometimes felt depressed, because, you know, you are sitting at home alone with this kid, who is supposed to … I mean who is a human being, but it is not a social contact who gives you the opportunity to talk, like really talk, you know? You can kind of meet with other mothers, but it doesn't really work like that. Because every child sleeps differently. So you can try twelve o'clock, but then my child sleeps at twelve. Then there is this period when everybody is ill. You try to meet up for two months but something always goes wrong. [C2W3 Ola]

> I had this feeling of claustrophobia, being closed up at home. And for me it's important that something is going on all the time, to have this feeling that I'm doing something important […]. Because I think it's important that at work you meet other people […]. Contact with a living human being who can talk to you is important, and I missed that. I also missed the fact that others treated me like a human being, not only like a mother. [C11W13 Sylwia]

The feeling of loneliness was accompanied with tiredness and a sense of powerlessness. Especially mothers of small babies suffered from sleep deprivation and a constant feeling of being tired. The concentration on a child, who needs constant attention, made it difficult to engage in other domestic duties or to just take a rest.

> I simply feel tired of this daily life, of being alone with children. For a whole week from nine in the morning to six in the evening I'm alone. I'm so happy when my husband comes back from work, that I can hand these responsibilities over to him. Although I know I can't put everything on him because he's also tired from paid work. [C19W27 Róża]

> I feel a bit down at home. I am sitting at home and there's this mess, I can't handle it and the kid wants something. I mean obviously we play and he's funny and loveable, but you hear about this [postnatal] depression [...]. And it is like for the tenth time he wants something from you, and you are just staying home. You know, this is total powerlessness. In a sense I really want to go out, but I can't go out. [C2M2 Kamil]

What is more, taking care of children requires patience and involvement in activities that are not very interesting for adults.

> It's very difficult ... because at least my experience of being a parent is that, let's say that I have five hours with children, I just can't do something with them for five hours. Sometimes I need a break. And in my opinion, that's not bad, because they [two daughters] can play with each other. They don't need me all the time. [S1M2 Marek]

In the context of what Marek said it is important to understand that the situation of single parents, as well as those mothers who decided to take a break from paid work in connection with care work, is much more difficult than the situation of couples in which both parents are highly engaged in caregiving. When both parents are engaged in caregiving they can *take breaks* and consequently have more strength to spend time alone with their children when necessary. As I shall demonstrate in the next chapter, paid work can serve as such a break. Many parents, especially women after parental leave, emphasise that they take a rest at work. Paid work is often perceived as easier and more enjoyable than care work at home.

> I go to work and often relax there [laugh], right? It's much easier for me than being with a child, with a child who is sick every half an hour, has outbursts of anger or insists on something, for example, not wanting to go out. On the emotional level it's easier to go to [paid] work than to deal with these emotions with my child. [C17W23 Irena]

On the other side of the continuum, there are people who perceive the experience of caregiving as a great and precious time during which they establish a strong relationship with their children, learn new skills, as well as closely observe how their children develop. Yet it is clear that such narratives were less common or appeared after a chorus of complaints, so the researcher did not have the impression that caregiving is only difficult and cannot be fulfilling. The positive narratives of caregiving concentrate on the uniqueness of this experience and the fact that children are growing up and that similar moments would never happen again.

> Ok, let's be honest, each child can always make its parent tired, but this time [six months on parental leave], well, I recall it as fantastic, in fact it was the time when my daughter was developing very fast, I was sitting with her, I saw as she was maturing, as she was changing every day, I don't know, she was saying new words and so on. So this time was very precious. [C7M8 Stefan]

## 3.4 "I'm a Bit Down…". Loneliness and Exhaustion in Care Work

In some narratives parents also noticed that staying at home with a child was a kind of rest from their paid work. For women this period of rest started when they were still pregnant but had stopped paid work. In the case of men this rest took place when they decided to go on parental leave for a longer period. As Piotr was saying about his three month parental leave.

> It was pretty great. What's more I rested from my work, in a mental sense, I was not thinking about my work, and that had never happened before … I've been working in the same place for the last six years, even more, so … I've never had so much time off work before, previously … well, maximum period of work I missed was two weeks, right? It was such a refreshing experience for me. [C13M14 Piotr]

The questions arising from this analysis are: why do so few parents focus on the positive aspects of care work? Why is caregiving perceived as such demanding and tiring work, whereas its rewarding aspect is hardly ever mentioned? There are a few assumptions that might help us to answer these questions. First, there is a need to see who complains about care work and who perceives it as a great experience. The positive experiences are more often expressed by people who just temporarily took a break from paid work to take care of their children. They are especially fathers, who took a few months of parental leave (but not all). This suggests that care work is experienced as pleasant and rewarding work when it is done temporarily. The gender dimension is also important here—for men care work is not an obligation that is imposed on them. Of course, as fathers they have some kind of obligation towards their children, but they are more connected with breadwinning rather than day-to-day caregiving. Men are perceived as secondary caregivers, whose role is to support the mother in her daily duty of care (Suwada 2017a). Therefore, if they take care of their children on a daily basis, it is rather a matter of their individual choice than an obligation imposed by society or some external circumstances. The issue of choice is quite important here—it recurs very often in different discussions on the non-transferrable part of parental leave reserved for fathers. People who are against such mechanisms often stress that parents should have a right to choose how they want to share their parental leave (Suwada 2017b). Such an approach also appeared in the interviews analysed here—people dislike being forced to do particular things either by the state or by an individual person. A similar conclusion may be drawn from analysis of unemployed housewives, who sometimes have a feeling of being externally forced to provide care work for children and other family members (Tomescu-Dubrow et al. 2019). It can be assumed that people who feel their actions result from their own choices are more content with their situation. Thus it is important to look at the issue of care work through the lens of gender, and recognise that the right to choose, with its consequent opportunity structures, is much more restricted for women.

The second issue is the low value society affords to care work. Care work is not recognised by the system as work. Many mothers who took a break from paid work in connection to motherhood have a feeling of being invisible to the system, other people and society in general. The feelings of Elwira, who is the stay-at-home mother of a child with severe disabilities, are a good illustration of invisibility and lack of recognition.

> I: The fact that I don't work, don't work for pay, that I don't have work which I go to from home ... because for him [her husband] it's easy, he goes out, then he comes back and he has a feeling that he was at work, he earned some money. Did something. And me? I'm staying at home and just doing nothing, am I?
> R: So do you have a feeling that your work is undervalued?
> I: I mean, this is not what I meant that it's undervalued, because she's my child. I do it ... I love her, so I don't look at this in such terms, but sometimes ... people around ... it's like with housewives, you know? People also say that they do nothing. And these women from morning to evening plan what to cook, what to clean. I have more obligations than such a housewife, but ... it's definitely very hard work. And the problem isn't that people underestimate me, but that they in general have no idea how my work is done. People have no idea what it's like to take care of a severely ill person at home. [P20K29 Elwira]

Elwira's experiences of care work are distinctly different from other parents—she needs to provide specialised care for her daughter with severe disabilities, yet even though her everyday schedule is full of various obligations, she still has an impression that she does *nothing*. Similar feelings are characteristic for other stay-at-home mothers, they feel that their efforts and all work done during the day are not recognised and appreciated by other people. They often have to deal with stereotypes of lazy housewives who unjustifiably take money from their husband or from the state (corresponding conclusions can be drawn from the experiences of unemployed mothers see: Karwacki and Suwada 2020). Such a situation is especially difficult when becoming a housewife is not a result of free-choice, but rather a consequence of various external conditions (see also: Tomescu-Dubrow et al. 2019).

## 3.5 Conclusion

Kaja Kojder-Demska (2015) notes that motherhood is not a matter of individual choice and individual experience, but it is rather an area in which different ideas and norms clash and come into conflict. This also applies to how care work is organised. Parents' choice is limited by opportunity structures that result from cultural norms and values, welfare state instruments, and labour market requirements. The organisation of care work is not merely a matter of the personal preferences of parents. The length of time available to stay at home with a child is limited by the length of available parental leave and is connected with the level of replacement rates and parents' economic resources. The organisation of care after a period of leave is constrained by the availability of places in childcare institutions, the availability of other family members who can give support in providing care, and by economic resources that can be used to buy care in the private sector. The experiences of Polish parents clearly indicate that economic inequalities are one of the most important dimensions that differentiate parents' opportunity structures. Yet regardless of economic resources mothers are always perceived as the main caregivers. The opportunity structures for men and women are distinctly different. The gendered norm about care is also present in the Polish family policy system that is explicitly genderising and promotes the traditional model of the family in which men are mainly responsible for breadwinning whereas women are responsible for care work. Consequently, women feel a bigger pressure to provide everyday care to their children, even if it has negative consequences for their other obligations. Men see themselves as helpers who support their partners or wives. At the same time, care work, even though it can be rewarding, is perceived as troublesome and boring. It brings more satisfaction if it results from a caregiver's individual choice than if it is imposed by external factors.

To understand prevailing gender inequalities, it is necessary to start with analysis of care work. Even though care is one of the most fundamental types of work for a society, it is undervalued. Its importance often goes unrecognised, since it is difficult to translate its everyday results into economic value. The gendered division of work and the perception of care work as a female obligation is still visible in Polish society despite changing gender roles and despite the increasing involvement of men in family life. Such a situation has an effect not only on the organisation of care work but also, as I show in the following chapters, on the organisation of paid work and domestic work.

## References

Brandth, B., & Kvande, E. (2016). Masculinity and fathering alone during parental leave. *Men and Masculinities*. https://doi.org/10.1177/1097184X16652659.
Caetano, A. (2015). Defining personal reflexivity: A critical reading of Archer's approach. *European Journal of Social Theory, 18*(1), 60–75. https://doi.org/10.1177/1368431014549684.
Dowd, N. E. (2000). *Redefining fatherhood*. New York University Press.
Elliott, K. (2016). Caring masculinities theorizing an emerging concept. *Men and Masculinities, 19*(3), 240–259. https://doi.org/10.1177/1097184X15576203.
Farstad, G. R. (2015). Difference and equality: Icelandic parents' division of parental leave within the context of a childcare gap. *Community, Work & Family, 18*(3), 351–367. https://doi.org/10.1080/13668803.2014.965661.
Hanlon, N. (2012). *Masculinities, care and equality*. Palgrave Macmillan UK.
Ingólfsdóttir, E. S., & Gíslason, I. V. (2016). Gendered solutions to the care gap issue in Iceland. *NORA: Nordic Journal of Women's Studies, 24*(4), 220–233. https://doi.org/10.1080/08038740.2016.1241826.
Iwanowicz-Palus, G., & Bogusz, R. (2018). *Opinie młodych matek na temat laktacji i roli położnej w promowaniu karmienia piersią. Raport z badań*. Polskie Towarzystwo Położnych. http://www.ptpol.pl/images/obrazy/karmienie_mlekiem/Raport_2018-2019.pdf.
Javornik, J., & Kurowska, A. (2017). Work and care opportunities under different parental leave systems: Gender and class inequalities in northern Europe. *Social Policy & Administration, 51*(4), 617–637. https://doi.org/10.1111/spol.12316.
Karwacki, A., & Suwada, K. (2020). Doświadczenie bezrobocia a relacje rodzinne we współczesnej Polsce – perspektywa płci. *Studia Socjologiczne, 1*(236), 165–194. https://doi.org/10.24425/sts.2020.132455.
Kojder-Demska, K. (2015). Kobiety, mleko i polityka karmienia we współczesnej Polsce. In R. E. Hryciuk & E. Korolczuk (Eds.), *Niebezpieczne związki: Macierzyństwo, ojcostwo i polityka* (pp. 159–182). Wydawnictwa Uniwersytetu Warszawskiego.

Kubisa, J. (2014). *Bunt białych czepków: Analiza działalności związkowej pielęgniarek i położnych*. Wydawn. Naukowe Scholar.
Miller, T. (2011). *Making sense of fatherhood: Gender, caring and work*. Cambridge University Press.
O'Brien, M., & Wall, K. (Eds.). (2017). *Comparative perspectives on work-life balance and gender equality: Fathers on leave alone*. Springer International Publishing. https://doi.org/10.1007/978-3-319-42970-0.
Pfau-Effinger, B., & Rostgaard, T. (2011). Introduction: Tensions related to care in European welfare states. In B. Pfau-Effinger & T. Rostgaard (Eds.), *Care between work and welfare in European societies* (pp. 1–14). Palgrave Macmillan.
Ranson, G. (2015). *Fathering, masculinity and the embodiment of care*. Palgrave Macmillan UK. https://doi.org/10.1057/9781137455895.
Reimann, M. (2016). Searching for egalitarian divisions of care: Polish couples at the life-course transition to parenthood. In D. Grunow & M. Evertsson (Eds.), *Couples' transitions to parenthood: Analysing gender and work in Europe* (pp. 221–242). Edward Elgar Publishing.
Scambor, E., Bergmann, N., Wojnicka, K., Belghiti-Mahut, S., Hearn, J., Holter, Ø. G., et al. (2014). Men and gender equality: European insights. *Men and Masculinities, 17*(5), 552–577. https://doi.org/10.1177/1097184X14558239.
Suwada, K. (2015). Naturalisation of the difference. The experience of fatherhood in Sweden and Poland. *Studia Humanistyczne AGH, 2*(16), 141–155. https://doi.org/10.7494/human.2015.14.2.141.
Suwada, K. (2017a). *Men, fathering and the gender trap. Sweden and Poland compared*. Palgrave Macmillan.
Suwada, K. (2017b). "It was necessary at the beginning to make this whole revolution": Men's attitudes to parental leaves in Sweden and Poland. *Men and Masculinities, 20*(5), 570–587. https://doi.org/10.1177/1097184X17727571.
Suwada, K. (2020). Strategie organizacji opieki nad dziećmi w społeczeństwie polskim w perspektywie nierówności społecznych. *Przegląd Socjologii Jakościowej, 16*(2), 152–169. https://doi.org/10.18778/1733-8069.16.2.09.
Tomescu-Dubrow, I., Dubrow, J. K., Kiersztyn, A., Andrejuk, K., Kolczynska, M., & Slomczynski, K. M. (2019). *The subjective experience of joblessness in Poland*. Springer.

**Open Access** This chapter is licensed under the terms of the Creative Commons Attribution 4.0 International License (http://creativecommons.org/licenses/by/4.0/), which permits use, sharing, adaptation, distribution and reproduction in any medium or format, as long as you give appropriate credit to the original author(s) and the source, provide a link to the Creative Commons license and indicate if changes were made.

The images or other third party material in this chapter are included in the chapter's Creative Commons license, unless indicated otherwise in a credit line to the material. If material is not included in the chapter's Creative Commons license and your intended use is not permitted by statutory regulation or exceeds the permitted use, you will need to obtain permission directly from the copyright holder.

# Chapter 4
# Paid Work and Parenting

**Abstract** This chapter is devoted to the issue of paid work. Despite analyses dominating today that perceive paid work as an obstacle to parenting, I argue that paid work is an important obligation arising from parenthood. My analysis indicates that becoming a parent has consequences on how individuals perceive paid work. It becomes more important and there is a bigger focus on the level of earnings. Polish parents feel an enormous economic pressures in connection to having children. Yet the attitudes of men and women to paid work are different. In case of men there is a greater pressure to keep paid work and have a decent salary. Whereas women more often perceive paid work as a source of satisfaction. On the one hand, they also feel pressure to be active in the labour market and to bring money home, but on the other hand they confine more attention to the fact that paid work should be satisfactory. What is more, the chapter discusses these gender differences in the context of economic inequalities, as well as differences between the situation of single and coupled parents.

**Keywords** Paid work · Parenting · Gender roles · Mothering · Fathering · Poland

## 4.1 Is Paid Work a Part of Parenting?

On the one hand, paid work is often perceived as an obstacle for parental engagement. In societies based on a neoliberal economy, long working hours, as well as demanding professional duties, have a negative impact on family life and generate conflict between paid work and family life. Thus many family researchers who study parenthood focus on the reconciliation of parental obligations with those arising from being active in the labour market (to mention a few: Crespi and Ruspini 2016; Drobnič and Guillén 2011; Emslie and Hunt 2009; Fahlén 2012; Olah and Frątczak 2013). Most European family policies are intended to help people to combine paid work with having children (Gregory and Milner 2009). On the other hand, the model of an adult worker has become the dominant model of contemporary family life. The European Union aims to increase employment rates, and expects almost everyone to be involved in paid work in the labour market. This is connected with the reorientation of the European welfare state that started to put more pressure on the relation between employment and social provisions (Daly 2011; Lewis 2001; Lewis and Giullari 2006). Consequently, paid work is seen as an instrument of social inclusion. Lack of paid work, unstable employment and forced part-time employment can lead to social marginalisation and exclusion, as well as to poverty which makes it difficult to meet the basic needs of life (Kaźmierczak-Kałużna 2017; Kozek et al. 2017). My analysis is based on the assumption that the centrality of employment for both men and women is a crucial norm in contemporary European societies (Ruby and Scholz 2018). This has consequences for how parents fulfil their parental duties and engage in parenthood. As I shall demonstrate in this chapter, analysis of the interviews with Polish mothers and fathers suggests that even though obligations resulting from paid work can interfere in fulfilling parental duties, paid work as such is not an obstacle to parenthood. It is rather seen as a crucial aspect of life helping to fulfil basic human needs and as a necessary condition to have children. Having children pushes individuals to paid work (Kotowska 2014; Kurowska 2019). The reasons for it are clear—a family life is expensive. The more children in a family, the more expenses of everyday life and the greater need to engage in paid work. This was a recurring theme in most of the interviews regardless of the financial situation of the researched individual.

> It's clear that [parenthood] is also a financial issue, that it's necessary to have an appropriate level of finances, that I need to earn enough to be able to maintain my family. I think that I earn quite a lot, but we have so many expenses that what I earn is actually the minimum necessary to maintain all of these, pay off the mortgage, pay for kindergarten, and all that special food, classes and so on. [P5M6 Filip]

Other research also indicates that economic uncertainty and an unstable employment situation, for both full-time and temporary employment, have a negative impact on the fertility intentions of both men and women (Karwacki and Suwada 2020; Kurowska 2019; Sobotka 2017). The data from Social Diagnosis, which used the panel research technique to study the conditions and quality of life in Polish society between 2000 and 2015, shows that job insecurity and a lack of paid work are perceived as the most important barriers to childbearing (Kotowska 2014). Moreover, employment rates suggest that having children is positively correlated with having a paid job. The Eurostat data (see Table 4.1) indicates that in Polish society, the employment rates of childless people are much lower than parents. In the case of men, the more children the higher the employment rate, whereas in the case of women higher employment rates are characteristic for women having one child or two children. The only exception is women with three or more children, who are less often employed than childless women.[1] In this context, paid work cannot be perceived as an obstacle to parenting, but rather as its essential component or even

---

[1] The effect of family size on women's employment is not clear. Since studies show that there is no significantly negative effect in the post-socialist countries (Baranowska-Rataj and Matysiak 2016; Matysiak 2011), this low employment rate can probably be explained with some other factors than only number of children.

## 4.1 Is Paid Work a Part of Parenting?

**Table 4.1** Employment rate of adults by sex and number of children—Poland

|  |  | 2015 | 2016 | 2017 | 2018 |
|---|---|---|---|---|---|
| Men | No children | 67.3 | 69.2 | 71.5 | 73.0 |
|  | 1 child | 84.2 | 85.7 | 87.0 | 88.2 |
|  | 2 children | 89.5 | 90.4 | 91.2 | 92.1 |
|  | 3 children or more | 85.0 | 85.7 | 87.6 | 89.1 |
| Women | No children | 56.7 | 58.8 | 60.8 | 62.1 |
|  | 1 child | 70.7 | 71.4 | 72.1 | 74.5 |
|  | 2 children | 69.2 | 69.8 | 70.2 | 70.8 |
|  | 3 children or more | 58.3 | 56.5 | 57.5 | 58.1 |

Source: The EUROSTAT database—Labour Force Survey. Prepared by the author

condition to have a child (Kurowska and Słotwińska-Rosłanowska 2013). Thus in this analysis paid work is seen as one way of fulfilling parental roles besides care work.

As Carol Emslie and Kate Hunt noted (2009) paid work and work resulting from family obligations should not be conceptualised as separate domains. It is important to acknowledge that family and professional responsibilities spill over and sometimes are strictly connected to each other. Yet gender is an important structural dimension which determines how men and women reconcile paid work with family life, how they define their parental and working obligations and what they prioritise. As shown in the previous chapter, care norms clearly expect women to provide care for their family members. This is strictly connected with the gendered structure of the labour market. To adequately describe the dynamics of gender relations in the context of paid work in Polish society, I refer to how they looked during the communist era. As Małgorzata Fidelis noted 'gender differences remained a primary way of demarcating and understanding social hierarchies in post war Poland' (Fidelis 2010, p. 2). Even though in the 1950s the communist government encouraged women to be active in the labour market and to take jobs that were traditionally reserved for men, gender differences still persisted in the division between public and domestic spheres. Consequently, the paid work of men and women was not treated with the same respect. Women's paid work was secondary and was legitimised only when it was necessary for the family, i.e. in the case of single, especially widowed, mothers or wives of unemployed or low earning men (Fidelis 2010; Jarska 2019, 2020). A similar conclusion was reached by Elizabeth Dunn, who was doing participatory research on women working in a baby food canning factory in the south of Poland in the 1990s.

> For many working mothers, wage labor is a sacrifice that one makes for one's children, in order to 'invest' in them. In this sense, wage labor is another way of providing children not only with tangibles such as food, which they need for growth, but also with intangibles like violin lessons, the all-important English lessons, or a costly private course at one of the now ubiquitous 'schools of management'. (Dunn 2004, p. 146)

Dunn observed that women working in the factory did so because of their family obligations, not because their paid work was a source of fulfilment. Many of them

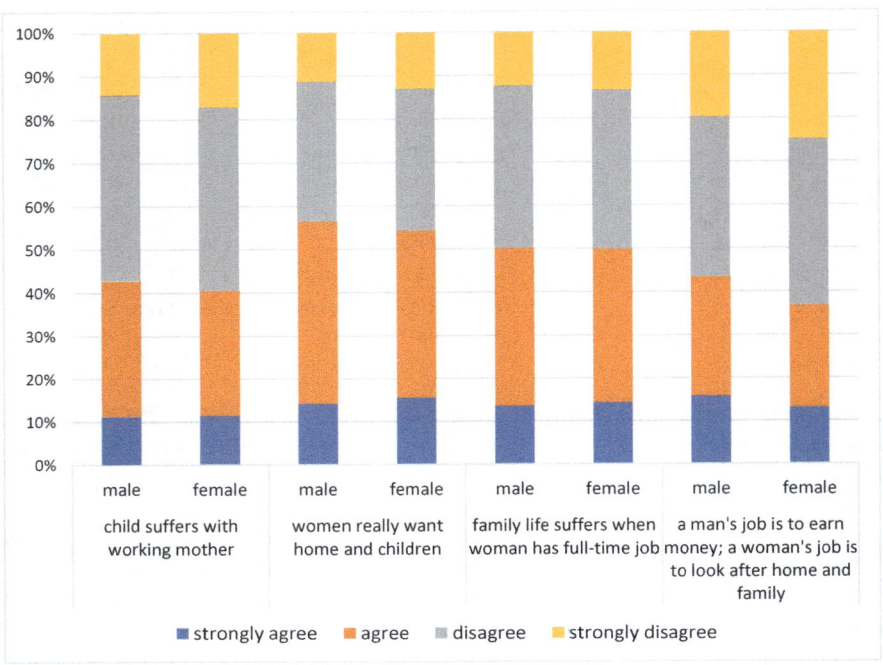

**Graph 4.1** Attitudes to women's participation in the labour market. Source EVS 2017. Prepared by the author

were forced to engage in paid work, because they had unemployed husbands, were single mothers and/or had large families to support. Dunn also shows that those women who had children believed that their employment was more important than did childless women whose labour 'went to frivolities and self-indulgences like dogs' (Dunn 2004, p. 147).

A different approach to the paid work of mothers and fathers is also observed in contemporary Polish society. Małgorzata Sikorska (2019) in her research on parental and family practices shows that a father's care and responsibilities are much more often seen as financial provision for children and family, as well as taking care of family finances. In the case of women, financial provision is rather seen in terms of *support* and her salary is *additional* to the father's salary (Sikorska 2019, pp. 232–237). The mixed approach to women's participation in the labour market is also visible in the European Value Survey. In 2017 several questions that illustrate this issue were asked. In Graph 4.1 it is shown that more than 56% of Poles (56.6% of men and 63% of women) disagree or strongly disagree with the statement 'A man's job is to earn money; a woman's job is to look after home and family'. What is more, 50% of people disagree with the statement that 'family suffers when a woman has a full-time job', as well as with the statement that 'a child suffers with a working mother'. This means that for many people women's paid work is acceptable and reasonable, yet there is still a huge percentage of Poles who prioritise men's paid work.

In Polish society there are mixed approaches to women's participation in the labour market and what impact it has on the family. In the following analysis, I look closely on how paid work was perceived by the interviewed parents.

## 4.2 "It's Clear That It's Also a Financial Issue...". The Necessity of Paid Work

The above mentioned questions that were asked in the European Value Survey in 2017 (EVS 2019) (but also in earlier waves) only concerned the impact of women's paid work on family life. There were no questions about whether the family suffers when a man has a full-time job or if what men really want is home and children, even though men are also parents, and as parents have various obligations and engage in various family practices. It might be assumed that in the opinion of the researchers preparing the survey questionnaire such questions are only relevant in the case of women. Women's paid work is more problematic for family life than men's paid work. This shows that as a society we differently problematise men's and women's engagement in paid work. The research on fatherhood clearly shows that even in times of changing gender roles and new models of fatherhood, being a good father still means being a breadwinner who can economically provide for his family (Bryan 2013; Pustułka et al. 2015; Ranson 2001; Suwada 2017). Many studies indicate that even though men are becoming more engaged in care and domestic work, they still do much less than women (Fuwa 2004; Kuhhirt 2012; Miller 2011; Suwada 2017; Titkow et al. 2004). Consequently, it can be assumed that for men having a child is a smaller obstacle to paid work than it is for women.

In Poland breadwinning is the main obligation for fathers. In 2017 when these in-depth interviews were conducted the employment rate of men with at least one child was 88.6%, whereas for childless men only 71.5%.[2] All interviewed fathers were active in the labour market, although their situations differed in terms of type of employment, salaries, occupation, as well as work stability. In the case of women participation in the labour market was less common, but still the majority of interviewed mothers worked full-time, and those who did not work usually planned to find a job. The only reason for interviewed mothers to remain unemployed was because of extraordinary circumstances, such as having children with severe disabilities. Yet it does not mean that men were to the same extent engaged in other parenting obligations, such as care work (see Chap. 3) and domestic chores (see Chap. 5). In general, the interviewed parents can be divided into two groups. On the one hand, there are people who follow the dual-earner/one-carer model, in which the role of a father is solely to economically provide for the family, whereas a mother is

---

[2]Source: Eurostat's Labour Force Survey.

responsible for care and domestic work while usually working full-time in the labour market. On the other hand, there are families which try to share all the obligations and realise (sometimes successfully) the model of dual-earner/dual-carer.

In both of these models, expectations for men are higher with regard to paid work—they are always supposed to be active in the labour market and are expected to bring money home. Whereas even though women's paid work is often necessary and desirable, it is more acceptable when a woman takes a break from paid work or decides to reduce her working hours. In the interviews mothers much more often said that at some point they considered taking a break from paid work, in the case of fathers such declarations were made very rarely. What is more, men still statistically earn more than women. According to Eurostat in 2017[3] the gender pay gap stood at 7.2% based on average gross hourly earnings. The interviewed parents often underlined that in their families the man earns more and/or holds a better and more stable position in the labour market.

> I: Whose [paid work] is more important? I don't know, I guess mine.
> R: Why?
> I: Because it brings better financial results. [C12M13 Mikołaj]

> I think that if I had to try to make an evaluation, then my husband's work is still more important – we even talked about it, because we mainly make a living from it and it gives some kind of stability. My job ... either I have it, or I don't, so it is often the case that we adjust to some things, because of his work. [C17K23 Irena]

The necessity of paid work together with financial issues were often raised in the interviews, regardless of the economic situation of the family. It seems that even parents with a good working situation and an average salary still have to manage their finances carefully (for more detailed analysis see: Olcoń-Kubicka 2016, 2020). The interviewed parents felt that they were under financial pressure and directly linked it to parenthood.

> And you know, every time you're thinking about having a kid, you need to simply earn lots of money! [C2W3 Ola]

> And yes, there's a greater pressure to earn money, but it's also connected with a mortgage, because it was linked to ... we took out a mortgage and when the house was ready, our youngest son was one week old and we moved in [...]. So there is this greater pressure that you can't quit your job and do whatever you want. It's connected with the fact of having children, but also with the fact of having a mortgage and a wife, who, of course, expects that you are a practical man who earns money [C5M6 Filip]

The need to have a job with good earnings is especially evident in the case of single parents, in particular those who do not receive regular maintenance or other support from the second parent. In their cases, having only one salary increases the feeling of insecurity and fear of losing their job.

---

[3]Source: Eurostat database, available at: https://ec.europa.eu/eurostat/data/database (accessed: 17-04-2020).

## 4.2 "It's Clear That It's Also a Financial Issue'.... The Necessity of Paid Work

But I have a child ... nobody pays my bills for electricity, my rent, or tuition for a kindergarten, right? All these kind of things are on me and it stresses me out a bit, you know? [S3W6 Iwona]

[My financial situation] is very bad. Spending per month ... is really something else. We have a mortgage for a house, which my wife doesn't pay, because a bailiff blocked her bank account (...). The mortgage is 1,660 PLN and I pay it. I also pay 2,100 PLN to rent a flat, plus around 1,000 PLN of additional payments. So that's 5,000 PLN per month, but my salary is only 2,100 PLN. So I take additional jobs. [S13M23 Maciej, who is in the process of divorce]

At the beginning I was afraid of losing my job, you know looking for a new job again ... I'm the only one who is earning for him [his son]. I have to think about money, about having everything we need at home so we can function normally. [S12M22 Robert]

It is important to recognise that paid work is one of the most fundamental types of work associated with parenthood. On the one hand, as I argued above, a lack of paid work is perceived as a serious obstacle to childrearing—people start to think about having children when their labour market situation is stable and guarantees steady earnings. On the other hand, having children has an impact on how people perceive their paid work and what attitudes they have towards their current working situation. Some interviewed parents emphasised that they could not quit their jobs easily any more, any plans of changing job would require careful consideration and planning so they would not end up unemployed. They also attached more importance to how much they earned.

R: Did your attitude to paid work somehow change after becoming a mum?
I: I mean, for sure I want to earn more money, among other things. Because a child costs, of course we could lower our standards of living. But my parents are quite well off, so I'm also used to better standards [...]. Fortunately, I can't complain, because my husband earns really well, so it gives us some kind of security, but you know, the situation in the labour market isn't stable. So I'd like to earn more, because I'm aware that we have different commitments and if something happens, we can't make a living out of one salary. [P4K5 Ela]

I: When it comes to responsibility, you know, it's not like that any more ... that I can earn this and that and it'd be enough for cigarettes and other things ... but there is an economic pressure ... economic pressure ... maybe rather a challenge, so I need to earn more than I used to.
R: So you feel that you have to earn more because there are more people in the household?
I: I mean, yes, more ... You know we did not need this apartment before, for two of us. But as a family we need it, don't we? [P3M4 Paweł]

Serious concerns about money are often reinforced by dept. The issue of repaying a mortgage arose in many interviews, of who earns enough to be recognised by a bank as able to regularly repay loan instalments. This is connected with a poor housing policy in Poland and a lack of affordable housing available for a family with average earnings. Polish parents have limited possibilities when looking for a home for their family. They can live with their parents, rent a place on the free market (which is very expensive) or take out a mortgage on a new house or flat. Social housing is usually out of reach, since it is available only for the poorest families. Consequently, one of the most common strategies for young parents is to get into debt to create a good home for their family.

The interviewed mothers and fathers expressed similar opinions on the matter of household finances. One result of the heavy financial pressure upon Polish families is women's greater participation in the labour market. Yet there are significant gender differences in how paid work is perceived. As Natalia Jarska notes: 'The professional engagement of married women and mothers was becoming widespread and 'normal'. Public opinion was still divided, as many considered the male breadwinner model as appropriate, but 'real life' didn't leave doubts that women should work.' (Jarska 2020, p. 9). In the following section I concentrate on the differing attitudes to paid work held by Polish parents according to gender.

## 4.3 "I Think That a Guy Should Earn to Support His Family". The Different Attitudes to Paid Work of Mothers and Fathers

Jarska (2020) in her analysis of men's role in family life during the 1960s and 1970s in Poland claims that men's domination at home was reshaped during state-socialism. Men's position as economic providers was weakened because of women's greater participation in the labour market, but at the same time their domination did not vanish, but 'was becoming more indirect and unstable' (Jarska 2020, p. 10). My previous research on fatherhood conducted in 2012 and 2013 showed that for Polish men breadwinning is still a central obligation connected to fatherhood (Suwada 2017). Since then the situation has not changed. The interviewed men often perceive their paid work as a crucial source of economic resources for the family. Whereas women's paid work is often perceived as help or additional income, but it is not perceived as the main source of income. A good illustration of such an approach is the two following quotations:

> I think I have such an approach that a man needs to earn money and support his family. I don't mind if my wife stays home. But she says that she's bored at home, that she'd like to go out and meet people, so she has a job now. [C12M13 Mikołaj]

> With my partner we had a deal that I'd find a job as late as possible, because we really wanted to be with our kids. We were guided by the idea of attachment parenting and we didn't want to hire a nanny or send children to nurseries ... but we couldn't afford it because we lived very modestly and we preferred to live like that rather than paying a nanny and me ... sitting in some ... I couldn't find a satisfying job, I didn't have any experience or connections. I'd end up as a cashier or something, which isn't satisfying or developing. [S6W18 Ada – about a situation before a break up]

In my sample there were no unemployed men. Other research on the experience of unemployment from 2017 showed that the lack of a job for one parent had a profound impact on family relations (Karwacki and Suwada 2020; Posłuszny et al. 2020). Unemployment is especially difficult for men, who have problems with finding new roles and identities in family life. In our analysis of family relations (Karwacki and Suwada 2020), we distinguished three types of men experiencing

## 4.3 "I Think That a Guy Should Earn to Support His Family". The Different Attitudes...

long-term unemployment: (1) housewives in trousers, (2) deadbeat fathers and (3) prodigal sons. Types one and two apply to men who are fathers. *Housewives in trousers* are men who overtook traditionally female obligations connected to domestic and care work. They encounter great difficulties in finding a main role outside of breadwinning. Lack of ability to economically provide for a family is for them humiliating and embarrassing. They have great difficulty developing their male identity based on care and domestic duties, and have a sense of being redundant. In the second type called *deadbeat fathers* unemployment leads to the breakup of family relationships. The deadbeat fathers are usually divorced (and the divorce is usually a result of losing a job) and do not sustain contact with their children. In the last type, *prodigal sons,* unemployment is a barrier to starting a family. *Prodigal sons* are usually young men who cannot find a job after finishing education and are forced to live with their elderly parents in family houses. Because of lack of economic resources they have problems sustaining stable relationships with their girlfriends and cannot make decisions about starting their own families. The comparisons between men and women experiencing long-term unemployment show that the lack of a job has a destructive impact on men and their family relationships, whereas for women it pushes them even more strongly towards care and domestic work, this makes them dependent on other family members. Women's unemployment is often functional for the rest of the family, because it helps to fill the care gap resulting from the lack of institutional care for children, as well as for the elderly and people with disabilities. Yet, similarly as in my research with parents, women experiencing joblessness are willing to return to the labour market and make an effort to find adequate paid work.

On the one hand, we can see that staying at home can be one of the strategies of organising everyday life that is seriously taken into consideration. And many of the interviewed mothers actually spent some prolonged period of time outside the labour market either becoming unemployed or on unpaid extended leave. This never happened to men, who rarely decided to take time off work even on paid parental leave (see Chap. 3 for more on men taking parental leave). On the other hand, parents' narratives often indicate that the decision of returning to paid work after a period of staying at home was not just a result of economic pressures (see also: Reimann 2016). Paid work is not only perceived as a source of income which is necessary for a family, but in the case of many women it is something more. For many mothers paid work is perceived as a *break* from care duties.

> Before, paid work was the most important, so when it comes to [paid] work, there was some kind of revaluation. When my son was born the family became the most important. I have no doubts about it, but there was also this change that when I go to work I take a rest there [laugh], because it's much easier than staying with a child all the time. [C17K23 Irena]

> He started parental leave, I went back to [paid] work and it was such a rest, you know? That you're sitting at your desk drinking coffee and looking at your computer. [C2W3 Ola]

Or as a source of satisfaction:

> Paid work was always important for me, it still is important, because I have this need for job satisfaction, satisfaction from doing things. That is why I wanted to get back to [paid] work, because after staying ten months at home I was exhausted. I'm definitely not a person who fulfils herself with staying home with a kid and taking care of domestic duties. [C11K13 Sylwia]

The parents' narratives clearly show that women's paid work is highly acceptable and by many men desirable. Even though Polish fathers feel the burden of being the main breadwinner in the family, they often expect their partners to participate in the labour market. On the one hand, this expectation is often a result of economic pressures and the impossibility of living on only one wage in contemporary Poland. Yet on the other hand, many interviewed men recognise that women's paid work has a positive impact on their relationships and family life in general.

> I think this one year is ok, when my partner is with our child. But I think that both parents need to work normally. I mean I don't put pressure on [my wife] to take whatever job she can find. But I think it's important to keep an eye on job offers. It's better to have continuity on the labour market, to be active. [C15M16 Witold]

> I mean the situation in which one parent spends most time at home, and the second is out for at least eight hours a day ... in my case it was much more, because I had a job which involved a lot of business trips, [this situation] causes a lot of tension, because on the one hand there's this sense of injustice that there are more duties on my shoulders, because you don't see the other person working [...]. Our marriage worked much better when my wife was working, even if it was just a few hours a day. [S8M17 Zbigniew]

> I: I really wanted my wife to get back to work immediately after maternity leave.
> R: Why?
> I: Because I think otherwise she would be very unhappy. This was my impression. Of course, I didn't force her or anything. I'm just not sure if I wanted to be with a person, who stays at home. [C1M1 Kuba]

The approach of these fathers indicates that the paid work of their partner is not only considered in terms of economic provision. It is seen as an important aspect of everyday life, which is important from a long-term perspective. The institutional arrangements of the welfare state are so organised to make unemployment an unprivileged position. Long-term inactivity in the labour market has a negative effect on a person's right to different social benefits, such as pensions, sick benefit and so on. This also leads to greater dependency on other family members. Furthermore, for the female interviewees the role of paid work is not only perceived in terms of economic necessity, but it is also a source of satisfaction that allows for personal development (similar conclusions are drawn by Reimann 2016).

> Paradoxically, I think this work became more important than before. But not in a sense that it's more time consuming, but in qualitative terms that I care more if this paid work is satisfactory for me. If I sacrifice my child for this work, then it must be worth it, you know? It's not only about paying the rent, but it should actually give me some pleasure. [C1W1 Jola]

## 4.3 "I Think That a Guy Should Earn to Support His Family". The Different Attitudes...

> I believe that everyone should have a chance to do what is fulfilling for them. And if it gives you money, it is also important. Because we do not solely exist to raise children and make money to support a family and pay a mortgage, we also need self-development. I'm quite satisfied with my job. I think I'm quite good at what I do. [C5W7 Anna]

Additionally, some women stressed that paid work is important because it gives them a feeling of independence from their husband/partner and the welfare state. Similar conclusions are drawn from the previously mentioned research on the experience of unemployment (Karwacki and Suwada 2020).

> I used to feel that if I don't have my own money that I earned from paid work, then I have less rights at home. It's difficult to explain, but there's this feeling, and I think many women have it. [C17W23 Irena]

> I'd like to overcome my depression and to be independent and earn money. Because it hurts the most. It hurts that I'm on benefits and feel worse than working people. I don't need a husband to be happy. I just want to work and not have to worry about anything. [S10W26 Justyna]

Such thinking about achieving fulfilment from paid work along with a feeling of being independent, is entirely missing from the narratives of fathers. Men think about paid work as something obvious that they have to do if they have children. They do not ponder if their paid work is satisfying or if it gives them a feeling of independence. It might be assumed that, on the contrary, they feel they have to work, because other people depend on them. This suggests that because of the traditional model of fatherhood based on breadwinning, fathers cannot just resign from paid work when it is unsatisfactory. They need to be active in the labour market regardless of the situation in their workplace or their sense of fulfilment.

This is not the only difference between the perception of paid work of mothers and fathers. The interviewed women whose children were not older than eight, generally did not think about making a career when their children still required more care and attention. On the one hand, it is clear that they want to have a satisfactory job, so they do not feel guilty for leaving a small child at home with another caregiver or in a nursery. On the other hand, they often stress that they cannot have paid work which is too demanding and time-consuming because they need to be able to fulfil other parental obligations (Sarnowska et al. 2020).

> You know, recently I was thinking about my career, because my boss is leaving and nobody has applied for her position yet, so I thought that maybe I could replace her. But no, not now because it would have consequences for my private life, and I can't do it because of the children. They are too small for me to do overtime. I mean I could hire a baby-sitter to pick them up from school or preschool, but I decided that I don't want to waste this time, that they are small and they need a mum at home, not a mum-boss. [S2W2 Ewa]

> Myself as every ... maybe not every ... but most women, I guess, we're managers of our own homes. So ... in a way it would be difficult to deal with more ambitious tasks at work. Because I manage our home, I manage our family time, and it's stressful in a way, so I have to postpone my professional ambitions for now. [C5W7 Anna]

In this context, the narratives of women with different levels of expertise are becoming quite similar. Even though women with unskilled jobs more often quit their paid work than women with skilled jobs (see Chap. 3), they usually intend to return to the labour market.

> R: Are you going to look for a job somewhere here?
> I: Yes, in [name of location]. And I want only one shift, you know? One shift so I could pick them up [children] from a kindergarten or something. So I could take them to a kindergarten and then pick them up. Yeah.
> R: Is it possible to find such a job here?
> I: Yes, it is. My friend works in such a job. The salary isn't high, but it's ok. (P9K11 Iza)

Women with low skills who need to continue paid work after a period of leave, usually make a deal with their employers and change their working conditions (for example, working on only one shift, reducing working hours, or not working at the weekend).

> I: My employer did me a favour, now I'll only work seven hours [per day]. It's less money, but only one shift and seven hours [instead of eight].
> R: And was it ok for him?
> I: Yes, I should work for eight hours [per day] and for two shifts. But he did me a favour. (S5K16 Maria)

Analysis of the interviews shows that the priorities of women in unskilled and/or low-paid jobs are similar to the priorities of other mothers—they want to have jobs that are not too time-consuming while at the same time letting them take a rest from the constant care of their children. Interestingly, for such women a lack of education or skills is rarely perceived as an obstacle to finding a job. Obstacles to being active in the labour market are more commonly seen as care obligations for their children and working conditions such as shift work or an inability to find part-time work (see also: Kaźmierczak-Kałużna 2017). In this context it is also important to recognise that women more often than men are in a precarious situation in the labour market, consequently women's paid work is often less stable, and women are at greater risk of becoming unemployed (Polkowska 2017; Posłuszny et al. 2020; Standing 2014).

## 4.4 "Time Is the Biggest Problem in My Life." Time Pressure in Parenting

The situation in the labour market is a key element that determines the opportunity structures of Polish parents. I shall now focus on the time pressures that are experienced by Polish parents. Studies on work and family life clearly show that both men and women feel time pressure resulting from the combination of paid work and parenthood. These two aspects of life, even though strictly connected to each other, often impose conflicting obligations upon individuals (Gauthier et al. 2004; van der Lippe et al. 2006; Roxburgh 2012; Sullivan 1997). The lack of time is also felt by Polish parents (Sikorska 2019). The main reason parents experience a deficit of time is paid work. In the Polish labour market most people work full-time, in 2017 when the interviews were conducted, part-time employment was only 6.3% of total employment (3.5% of male employment and 9.8% of female employment). These numbers are very low in comparison to other European countries. For the whole European Union (28 members including the UK) part-time employment was 18.7% (8.1% of male and 31.1% of female employment). Women are more often employed part-time to be able to combine paid work with the requirements of motherhood. The highest percentages of women working part-time are in Western-European countries such as the Netherlands, Austria or Germany. Whereas the lowest percentages are characteristic of post-communist countries such as Slovakia, Croatia, Hungary and Poland.[4] Such a situation has consequences for how men and women combine paid work with parental obligations. Susan Fahlén argues that in countries with less access to part-time work (and strong traditional gender roles) 'women are expected to be the prime carer and men the prime earner' (Fahlén 2014, p. 378). Consequently, Polish working mothers more often face the dilemma of quitting a job due to care obligations, and have less time during the day to take care of their children when compared to other European mothers. The aim of this chapter is to analyse how being a parent influences engagement in paid work, and conversely how working arrangements affect engagement in care work due to economic and gender inequalities. The biggest problems appear at the moment when a parent who was on parental leave (usually a mother) returns to paid work.

> Returning to work from maternity leave is like a blow to the head. Really. Because the time of leave is a period when you have the whole day and you can somehow sort out everything that needs to be done. And then [upon return to paid work] there are more duties but there is no time, because when you are eight hours at work, in fact ten hours, because of commuting ... and you think 'Oh my God, I have no time!'. [C4W5 Ela]

The moment of returning to paid work from a period of leave for one parent is a time when there is a need to set new schedules and determine new priorities. It has an impact on engagement in paid work. The narratives of interviewed parents, who work full-time, clearly show that paid work takes the most time in their daily life, usually one third of twenty-four hours. Despite this, the interviews indicate that in general time-consuming paid work is not prioritised by parents working full-time. The necessity of spending so much time at paid work is rather a result of the labour market conditions and the fact that part-time employment is not a popular solution in Poland. This is an important element which dictates parents' opportunity structures. The prioritisation of paid work is openly expressed by only a few of the interviewed parents. These are usually fathers who are motivated by economic pressures assigned to the traditional model of fatherhood or the fact that as young people they are at the beginning of their career path, which therefore requires greater focus on paid work. Yet interestingly, the current greater focus on paid work is usually connected with the necessity to provide good living conditions for the family, and

---

[4]Source: Eurostat database, available at: https://ec.europa.eu/eurostat/data/database (accessed: 22-04-2020).

sometimes it is even expected to bring positive long-term results, such as more time for the family in future. In such a case, long hours spent at paid work are described in the interviews as something done for the family, not for personal development.

> I think I spend more energy on my work than on my family. Obviously, I would like it to be the other way around, but this partly results from the fact that I believe that if I work hard now, then in a few years it'll be different. That in future I can go to work for three - four hours and, for example, spend more time at home with my children. [C15M16 Witold]

On the other hand, the prioritisation of paid work can also be a result of bad relations in the family, which is clearly visible in the narratives of single parents who went through a divorce.

> I really love my children, but . . . I didn't get on so well with my wife, so I was escaping from family life and my work was a perfect excuse. I had lots of delegations and didn't spend much time at home. But this was not because of any institutional conditions, but due to my relationship with my wife. I planned my paid work to be at home as little as possible. And now when we have finally decided to break up, it's resulted in a greater work/life balance. [S1M2 Marek]

In the sample of interviewed parents, only a few men clearly declared that their paid work is or used to be a priority. Women never made such a declaration. This does not mean that there are no mothers who prioritise paid work, yet it might be assumed that because of strong gendered norms around care it is more difficult for them to admit to this openly. In the context of time management, most of the interviewees with skilled jobs claimed that in connection to parenthood they changed their attitudes to paid work and working hours. Before becoming a parent, many of them did overtime, brought work home, worked during weekends or simply thought about work outside the office.

> [Paid work] stopped being so important. And this is something that childless people cannot understand, it's hard to talk about it with them. But . . . sometimes before I had a child, when there were stressful situations, important projects, something was going on at work and I was thinking about it all the time. I was back at home and I was thinking and living with it all the time. And now when I leave the office and am back home, I don't think about it, because I have plenty of other things to think about. [C11W13 Sylwia]

> R: Did something change when you became a father?
> I: Yes, I have less inclination to work sixteen hours a day. There are some constraints and I have to take it into consideration that there is another person who I'm responsible for, and I'd like to participate in her upbringing. Even though at the beginning I wasn't feeling competent enough to take care of her, but when she is older that I will participate more. This is how I see it. [P15M16 Witold]

Analysis of the interviews shows that regardless of the attitudes to gender roles in family life, attitudes to paid work are changing. I argue here that it is connected with time limits—new parents need to re-evaluate their approach to paid work because they simply have no time to solely concentrate on it. Time pressures not only affect how paid work is perceived by parents, but also how they deal with their work obligations. As mentioned above, parents try not to bring work home and do not work during weekends. This mostly applies to individuals who work outside the

## 4.4 "Time Is the Biggest Problem in My Life." Time Pressure in Parenting

household. The situation of parent-teleworkers is different, since they cannot easily isolate themselves from their children when they want to engage in paid work. They usually need to set some boundaries between time for paid work and time for other obligations (see: Gądecki et al. 2016, 2017), but the situation of having a small child at home makes this particularly difficult.

> It's difficult to be with a kid, but also to deal with everything that is beyond this relationship with my kid, I mean keeping the apartment in order, food and paid work ... and this frustration connected to paid work. I think it's inherent in my job and it's a nightmare. [P2M3 Kamil]

Some interviewees notice that their work from home became more structured and more effective since they are aware of time limits and cannot postpone certain duties.

> Before, I usually worked at night, and considered myself a typical night owl, but now it's different. But I'm also much more ... my work is more structured and I have no feeling that my day is falling apart. I mean, I just know what needs to be done and when to do it. I do more things immediately now, I procrastinate much less, basically it just doesn't happen [...]. I'm amazed by how much I can get done. And I don't think my child is suffering because of my workload. [C3W4 Joanna]

> Here's what I learned when I had my first son and was, you know, trying to work from home: as soon as he closed his eyes, I'd immediately sit at the computer. I didn't even check my Facebook or anything, I just started tapping away at the keyboard. You simply learn how to organise your time, how to maximise every moment without children [laugh]. [C2W3 Ola]

Obviously, not every parent has such experiences with organising time, but the interviews indicate that in general when becoming a parent, attitudes to the time management of paid work are changing, especially in the case of skilled workers. Parents with low-skilled work that is usually low paid do not mention such changes, although they more often look for additional work to earn some extra money. Since many of them do not have the option of taking work home, they usually work eight hours per day and do not think about their working obligations at home. They do overtime less often and it is easier for them to actually look for some additional work.

> No, I don't do overtime. I work eight hours, sometimes less. [C9M10 Jacek]

> For example, I was earning some extra money at weekends [working in a restaurant], so we had more money, but ... I don't have much experience in the kitchen, so they let me go. But now I'm looking for some weekend work. [C9W11 Iza]

Yet the relationship between parenthood and paid work can also be analysed from the perspective of how paid work affects everyday family life. In the interviews almost every parent complained about a lack of time. In the analysis of the interviews using the software programme MaxQDA the code 'lack of time' was used most often and was assigned to 45 out of 53 interviews. This lack of time results from the fact that parents usually have to work full-time so consequently have less time to spend at home and with the family. The time that remains after finishing paid work is usually devoted to a child. Parents prefer to neglect other domestic and family duties and concentrate on their children.

So when the weekend comes, it goes by so fast that [laugh] I need to choose, you know? Should I clean the flat or maybe take my kid out for a bike ride? So I choose the latter and go outside. I think that . . . I'm not allergic to dust, my child is not allergic to dust, so it can stay one more week. [S3W6 Iwona]

But many parents have a problem finding time to solely dedicate to their children, and those who have more than one child struggle to find time which is devoted to only one child.

> Basically, the problem is that the day is too short. Sometimes I'd like to finish certain things, but I can't. And I'd like to be there for them [the children] for at least a part of the day, but because I have so many duties, it's very difficult to find time when I'm focused only on them. (C14W19 Paulina)

> The problem isn't just that I have no time for myself, but also that I feel each of them would like to have me more. So they compete for my attention. I try to share my time fairly, but it's not possible. It's like whoever is screaming louder has my attention. [S2W3 Ewa]

In the above extracts Ewa mentioned that she has no time for herself. This is another problem experienced by most of the interviewed parents, especially mothers, who spend more time on domestic duties than fathers (this issue is discussed in Chap. 5). The interviewed mothers often noticed that they had difficulty finding time for themselves, but that their partner/husband didn't have such difficulties.

> It seems to me that we have less time now when we have a daughter, but also that [my husband] can still find time for himself - I envy him. For example, he plays computer games or learns programming, I can see that our daughter knows she cannot bother him when he's sitting at his computer. But when I'm sitting at my computer, she has no problem coming to me and asking for something. [C7W9 Stefa]

The perspective of fathers is a little bit different, even though they also complain about a lack of time, they more often see opportunities to find some time for themselves. They often stress that they do many things while commuting to work.

> I mean, this is an issue I was talking about with many people – we have as much time as we can find [. . .]. For example, I work out [at home] from 9 p.m. till 10.30 p.m. It's not a time when my presence is necessary [. . .]. And I always try to go to work by bike and come back by bike. It perhaps takes more time than by car, but I can cover 15 kilometres by bike this way. [C7M8 Stefan]

> I try to make the best use of my time when I don't have to take care of my son, if I have enough energy, you know. So I read on the bus when I go to work and come back . . . I don't feel I have much time, but on the other hand I don't feel any pressure. It's more like . . . I have some additional aspiration and I try to fulfil it in the 'meantime', let's say. [C13M14 Piotr]

The large amount of time that parents devote to paid work and care work has consequences for time organisation, including time spent with a partner. The interviewed parents often raised the problem of having no time for themselves as a couple. Sometimes they can get some help from other family members, especially the child's grandparents, who can take care of their children during an evening or a weekend, but it is not always possible and is a rather rare event.

R: Do you spend time with your wife, I mean without your child?
I: No.
R: No?
I: No, there is nobody who can take care of our daughter. Her grandmother lives 70 kilometres from us. She [the daughter] was there two or three times this summer, but I worked till the evening. [C10M11 Wojciech]

R: Are you able to spend time together, without the children?
I: Since our daughter [second child] was born, no.
R: And before?
I: Very rarely. In general, when our elder son went to his grandparents, we could, but only once he had grown up a bit. Then yes, but it was very rare. [C15M16 Witold]

Since Polish parents spend so much time on paid work, the time available for other obligations and everyday activities is limited. It is most difficult for parents with children of preschool age to find time for themselves individually and as a couple. Many parents think that such a situation is temporary, they believe that when their children grow up, they will regain more free time for themselves. Yet in this context it must be recognised that not only family policy, but also the labour market policy is crucial for parenting experiences in Polish society. In Poland there is a lack of mechanisms that would help parents to temporarily reduce their working hours in connection to parenthood. Consequently, parents (mostly mothers) who finish parental leave and return to the labour market have to deal with a substantial change in the everyday organisation of family life. At the same time, in the interviews many parents were talking about how working part-time could improve the quality of their everyday life. Many parents declare that they would love to reduce their working hours if it did not necessitate lowering their salary.

## 4.5 Conclusion

The importance of paid work is not questioned in an advanced capitalist society. Almost everyone is expected to work. Employment is seen as an instrument of social inclusion that allows for active participation in society (Lahusen and Giugni 2016; Tomescu-Dubrow et al. 2019). Consequently, engagement in paid work is one of the most common experiences for most people. At the same time, most people are also parents, and as parents they are involved in paid work. In this chapter I have argued that there is a need to stop perceiving paid work as an obstacle to parenting. Because of the requirements of the current economic system, paid work should rather be seen as one of the parental obligations. Individuals work for pay and keep their jobs because they have children. Individuals decide to have children if they have a satisfactory situation in the labour market. The conditions of the labour market and the situation of paid work of a particular individual are important factors that determine opportunity structures of a parent. They provide and at the same time limit an individual's opportunity to fulfil different parental obligations. Important dimensions here are gender and economic resources.

The situation of mothers and fathers are distinctly different. Even though both men and women are expected to work in the labour market, men feel greater pressure in connection with paid work. They more often perceive their parental obligations in terms of economic provision. This means that they feel greater pressure to keep a job and earn money. Paid work for fathers is not an obstacle, but rather a core parental obligation. Whereas in the case of women, paid work is more often regarded as secondary. They are more concentrated on other parental obligations, in particular those involving care, and consequently, more overtly experience time pressures as trying to combine paid work with care and domestic work. In this context it is necessary to recognise the role of the welfare state, which through different instruments of family policy help to reconcile different parental obligations. The Polish family system in the 2010s is based on explicit familialism (Szelewa 2017) and is explicitly genderising (Saxonberg 2014; Suwada 2017). This means that it promotes a traditional model of a family, in which men are focused on paid work, whereas women are more oriented on the domestic sphere. The experiences of Polish parents show that the reconciliation of different obligations arising from family life and paid work is very difficult mostly because of time pressure. In the Polish system there are no incentives which promote part-time employment or reduce working hours. Consequently, full-time paid work severely limits the opportunity structures of Polish parents.

## References

Baranowska-Rataj, A., & Matysiak, A. (2016). The causal effects of the number of children on female employment—Do European institutional and gender conditions matter? *Journal of Labor Research, 37*(3), 343–367. https://doi.org/10.1007/s12122-016-9231-6.

Bryan, D. M. (2013). To parent or provide? The effect of the provider role on low-income men's decisions about fatherhood and paternal engagement. *Fathering: A Journal of Theory, Research, and Practice about Men as Fathers, 11*(1), 71–89. https://doi.org/10.3149/fth.1101.71.

Crespi, I., & Ruspini, E. (Eds.). (2016). *Balancing work and family in a changing society: The fathers' perspective*. Palgrave Macmillan.

Daly, M. (2011). What adult worker model? A critical look at recent social policy reform in Europe from a gender and family perspective. *Social Politics: International Studies in Gender, State & Society, 18*(1), 1–23. https://doi.org/10.1093/sp/jxr002.

Drobnič, S., & Guillén, A. M. (Eds.). (2011). *Work-life balance in Europe: The role of job quality*. Palgrave Macmillan.

Dunn, E. C. (2004). *Privatizing Poland: Baby food, big business, and the remaking of labor*. Cornell University Press.

Emslie, C., & Hunt, K. (2009). 'Live to work' or 'work to live'? A qualitative study of gender and work–life balance among men and women in mid-life. *Gender, Work & Organization, 16*(1), 151–172. https://doi.org/10.1111/j.1468-0432.2008.00434.x.

EVS. (2019). *European Values Study 2017: Integrated Dataset (EVS 2017)* [ZA7500 Data file Version 2.0.0]. GESIS Data Archive; https://doi.org/10.4232/1.13314

Fahlén, S. (2012). *Facets of work-life balance across Europe: How the interplay of institutional contexts, work arrangements and individual resources affect capabilities for having a family and for being involved in family life*. Stockholm University and Stockholm University Library.

# References

Fahlén, S. (2014). Does gender matter? Policies, norms and the gender gap in work-to-home and home-to-work conflict across Europe. *Community, Work & Family, 17*(4), 371–391. https://doi.org/10.1080/13668803.2014.899486.

Fidelis, M. (2010). *Women, communism, and industrialization in postwar Poland.* Cambridge University Press.

Fuwa, M. (2004). Macro-level gender inequality and the division of household labor in 22 countries. *American Sociological Review, 69*(6), 751–767. https://doi.org/10.1177/000312240406900601.

Gądecki, J., Jewdokimow, M., & Zadkowska, M. (2016). Reconstructing the borders and the definitions of home and work in the context of telecommuting in Poland. *Intersections, 2*(3). https://doi.org/10.17356/ieejsp.v2i3.166.

Gądecki, J., Jewdokimow, M., & Żadkowska, M. (2017). *Tu się pracuje!: Socjologiczne studium pracy zawodowej prowadzonej w domu na zasadach telepracy.* LIBRON.

Gauthier, A. H., Smeeding, T. M., & Furstenberg, F. F. (2004). Are parents investing less time in children? Trends in selected industrialized countries. *Population and Development Review, 30*(4), 647–672. https://doi.org/10.1111/j.1728-4457.2004.00036.x.

Gregory, A., & Milner, S. (2009). Editorial: Work–life balance: A matter of choice? *Gender, Work & Organization, 16*(1), 1–13. https://doi.org/10.1111/j.1468-0432.2008.00429.x.

Jarska, N. (2019). Female breadwinners in state socialism: The value of women's work for wages in post-stalinist Poland. *Contemporary European History, 28*(4), 469–483. https://doi.org/10.1017/S0960777319000201.

Jarska, N. (2020). Men as husbands and fathers in postwar Poland (1956-1975): Towards new masculine identities? *Men and Masculinities.* https://doi.org/10.1177/1097184X20910492.

Karwacki, A., & Suwada, K. (2020). Doświadczenie bezrobocia a relacje rodzinne we współczesnej Polsce – perspektywa płci. *Studia Socjologiczne, 1*(236), 165–194. https://doi.org/10.24425/sts.2020.132455.

Kaźmierczak-Kałużna, I. (2017). Domowe menedżerki—Praca w opiniach wielodzietnych matek z ubogich rodzin. In E. Kolasińska, J. Róg-Ilnicka, & A. Mrozowicki (Eds.), *Praca w XXI wieku: Wymiary formalne i nieformalne* (Vol. 1–233–265). Wydawnictwo Naukowe Katedra.

Kotowska, I. (Ed.). (2014). *Niska dzietność w Polsce w kontekście percepcji Polaków. Diagnoza społeczna 2013 raport tematyczny.* Ministerstwo Pracy i Polityki Społecznej : Centrum Rozwoju Zasobów Ludzkich.

Kozek, W., Kubisa, J., & Zieleńska, M. (2017). *Utrzymać się na powierzchni: O walce z biedą w pięciu krajach europejskich w perspektywie indywidualnego sprawstwa.* Wydawnictwo Naukowe Scholar.

Kuhhirt, M. (2012). Childbirth and the long-term division of labour within couples: How do substitution, bargaining power, and norms affect parents' time allocation in West Germany? *European Sociological Review, 28*(5), 565–582. https://doi.org/10.1093/esr/jcr026.

Kurowska, A. (2019). Experienced and anticipated changes in household economic situation and childless women's short-term intentions to become mothers. *European Societies, 0*(0), 1–19. https://doi.org/10.1080/14616696.2019.1583357.

Kurowska, A., & Słotwińska-Rosłanowska, E. (2013). Zatrudnienie a pierwsze i drugie urodzenia wśród kobiet w Polsce. *Studia Demograficzne, 1*(163), 37–51.

Lahusen, C., & Giugni, M. (2016). Experiencing long-term unemployment in Europe: An introduction. In C. Lahusen & M. Giugni (Eds.), *Experiencing long-term unemployment in Europe— Youth on the edge* (pp. 1–16). Palgrave Macmillan UK.

Lewis, J. (2001). The decline of the male breadwinner model: Implications for work and care. *Social Politics: International Studies in Gender, State & Society, 8*(2), 152–169. https://doi.org/10.1093/sp/8.2.152.

Lewis, J., & Giullari, S. (2006). The adult-worker-model family and gender equality: Principles to enable the valuing and sharing of care. In S. Razavi & S. Hassim (Eds.), *Gender and social policy in a global context: Uncovering the gendered structure of 'the social'* (pp. 173–190). Palgrave Macmillan UK. https://doi.org/10.1057/9780230625280_8.

Matysiak, A. (2011). Fertility developments in Central and Eastern Europe: The role of work–family tensions. *Demográfia English Edition, 54*(5), 7–30.
Miller, T. (2011). *Making sense of fatherhood: Gender, caring and work*. Cambridge University Press.
Olah, L. S., & Frątczak, E. (Eds.). (2013). *Childbearing, women's employment and work-life balance policies in contemporary Europe*. Palgrave Macmillan.
Olcoń-Kubicka, M. (2016). Financial arrangement as a reflection of household order. *Polish Sociological Review, 196*(4), 477–494.
Olcoń-Kubicka, M. (2020). Pursuit of fairness in household financial arrangements among young middle-class couples in Poland. *Journal of Consumer Culture, 20*(2), 156–174. https://doi.org/10.1177/1469540519891272.
Polkowska, D. (2017). The feminisation of precarity Poland compared to other countries. *Annales. Etyka w Życiu Gospodarczym, 20*(8), 119–135. https://doi.org/10.18778/1899-2226.20.8.10.
Posłuszny, Ł., Karolak, M. P., & Kubicki, P. (2020). Stąpając po niepewnym gruncie. Prekaryjność i bezrobocie w pamiętnikach bezrobotnych Polek i Polaków. *Studia Socjologiczne, 236*(1), 223–256. https://doi.org/10.24425/sts.2020.132457.
Pustułka, P., Struzik, J., & Ślusarczyk, M. (2015). Caught between breadwinning and emotional provisions—The case of Polish migrant fathers in Norway. *Studia Humanistyczne AGH, 14*(2), 117. https://doi.org/10.7494/human.2015.14.2.117.
Ranson, G. (2001). Men at work: Change—Or no change? - In the era of the 'new father'. *Men and Masculinities, 4*(1), 3–26. https://doi.org/10.1177/1097184X01004001001.
Reimann, M. (2016). Searching for egalitarian divisions of care: Polish couples at the life-course transition to parenthood. In D. Grunow & M. Evertsson (Eds.), *Couples' transitions to parenthood: Analysing gender and work in Europe* (pp. 221–242). Edward Elgar Publishing.
Roxburgh, S. (2012). Parental time pressures and depression among married dual-earner parents. *Journal of Family Issues, 33*(8), 1027–1053. https://doi.org/10.1177/0192513X11425324.
Ruby, S., & Scholz, S. (2018). Care, care work and the struggle for a careful world from the perspective of the sociology of masculinities. *Österreichische Zeitschrift Für Soziologie, 43*(1), 73–83. https://doi.org/10.1007/s11614-018-0284-z.
Sarnowska, J., Pustułka, P., & Wermińska-Wiśnicka, I. (2020). Słabe państwo i solwatacja społeczna w obszarze łączenia pracy z rodzicielstwem. *Studia Socjologiczne, 237*(2), 135–162. https://doi.org/10.24425/sts.2020.132465.
Saxonberg, S. (2014). *Gendering family policies in post-Communist Europe: A historical-institutional analysis*. Palgrave Macmillan.
Sikorska, M. (2019). *Praktyki rodzinne i rodzicielskie we współczesnej Polsce—Rekonstrukcja codzienności*. Wydawnictwo Naukowe Scholar.
Sobotka, T. (2017). Childlessness in Europe: Reconstructing long-term trends among women born in 1900–1972. In M. Kreyenfeld & D. Konietzka (Eds.), *Childlessness in Europe: Contexts, causes, and consequences* (pp. 17–53). Springer. https://doi.org/10.1007/978-3-319-44667-7_2.
Standing, G. (2014). *The precariat: The new dangerous class* (Revised ed. edition). Bloomsbury Academic.
Sullivan, O. (1997). Time waits for no (wo)man: An investigation of the gendered experience of domestic time. *Sociology, 31*(2), 221–239. https://doi.org/10.1177/0038038597031002003.
Suwada, K. (2017). *Men, fathering and the gender trap. Sweden and Poland compared*. Palgrave Macmillan.
Szelewa, D. (2017). From implicit to explicit familialism: Post-1989 family policy reforms in Poland. In *Gender and family in European economic policy* (pp. 129–151). Cham: Palgrave Macmillan.
Titkow, A., Duch-Krzystoszek, D., & Budrowska, B. (2004). *Nieodpłatna praca kobiet: Mity, realia, perspektywy*. Wydawnictwo IFiS PAN.
Tomescu-Dubrow, I., Dubrow, J. K., Kiersztyn, A., Andrejuk, K., Kolczynska, M., & Slomczynski, K. M. (2019). *The subjective experience of joblessness in Poland*. Springer.

# References

van der Lippe, T., Jager, A., & Kops, Y. (2006). Combination pressure: The paid work: Family balance of men and women in European countries. *Acta Sociologica, 49*(3), 303–319. https://doi.org/10.1177/0001699306067711.

**Open Access** This chapter is licensed under the terms of the Creative Commons Attribution 4.0 International License (http://creativecommons.org/licenses/by/4.0/), which permits use, sharing, adaptation, distribution and reproduction in any medium or format, as long as you give appropriate credit to the original author(s) and the source, provide a link to the Creative Commons license and indicate if changes were made.

The images or other third party material in this chapter are included in the chapter's Creative Commons license, unless indicated otherwise in a credit line to the material. If material is not included in the chapter's Creative Commons license and your intended use is not permitted by statutory regulation or exceeds the permitted use, you will need to obtain permission directly from the copyright holder.

# Chapter 5
# Domestic Work and Parenting

**Abstract** This chapter deals with the last type of work distinguished in the beginning of the book—domestic work. Domestic work is often perceived as the most undesirable type of work. I describe here different attitudes of men and women to domestic work. My analysis shows great gender inequalities. Men are still perceived as helpers of women, whereas women are overwhelmed with the obligation to manage everyday life of their families. I distinguish different strategies used by men to avoid domestic duties, as well as women's attitudes to them. The chapter deals also with the concept of fairness. I show how parents define fairness and I argue that fairness does not have to mean equality in the division of domestic work. The chapter finishes with the strategies of reducing the number of hours devoted to domestic duties. It shows how that economic inequalities cannot be ignored when discussing this issue, as well as various situations of single and coupled parents.

**Keywords** Domestic work · Domestic help · Gender inequalities · Gender roles · Fairness · Poland

## 5.1 Prevailing Inequalities in the Household

In this chapter I concentrate on those domestic duties that to some extent are separate from care work and paid work. It is sometimes difficult to find a clear boundary between these types of work, especially between domestic work and care work, yet I claim here that it is important to categorise them differently in order to recognise the dynamics of gender inequality (Sullivan 2013). The interviewed parents also made a distinction between these different types of work. Domestic work is understood here as all activities done in connection to the household, such as cleaning, washing dishes, laundry, ironing, repairs and disposing of rubbish as well as shopping and preparing meals. The interviews indicated that this work is not valued as highly as care work or paid work. On the one hand, domestic work often has to be done in order to fulfil obligations resulting from other types of work. But on the other hand, it is easier to delegate to other people, delay or perform negligently. As has been argued, it is the most *undesirable* type of work (Bird and Ross 1993; Taniguchi and

© The Author(s) 2021
K. Suwada, *Parenting and Work in Poland*, SpringerBriefs in Sociology,
https://doi.org/10.1007/978-3-030-66303-2_5

Kaufman 2020). Similarly, as with care work, domestic work is traditionally assigned to women as a part of their everyday obligations resulting from gender roles (Kosakowska-Berezecka et al. 2018). Changing gender roles, in particular women's participation in the labour market, has challenged these traditional norms, and consequently, domestic work has now become an area of conflict and negotiation between couples (Hochschild and Machung 2003; Żadkowska 2016). Yet this does not mean that gender inequalities have dissolved. In fact, social research indicates that they still prevail, especially among couples with children (Coltrane 2000; Fuwa 2004; Kuhhirt 2012; Schober 2013; Solera and Mencarini 2018; Statistics Poland 2016). Becoming a parent results in a significant increase in domestic and care duties, as well as in a reinforcement of traditional gendered norms regarding everyday practices. As Carmen Sirianni and Cynthia Negrey note: 'Increases in total household-labor time, which result primarily from the presence of children (the more and the younger), lead to larger increases in the wives' than the husbands' contributions to such labor' (2000, p. 62). The reinforcement of traditional gender roles is also observable in Polish society (Reimann 2016, 2019; Titkow et al. 2004; Żadkowska 2016). This can be explained with prevailing models of motherhood and fatherhood that are based on strong gender norms, as well as the welfare state regime that reproduces gender inequalities. In Polish society, on the one hand, there is a high gender equity in individual-oriented institutions such as employment and education. A woman's right to participate in the education system and labour market is not questioned. On the other hand, family-oriented institutions are characterised by low gender equity. Such a situation leads to a bifurcation in how women perceive their obligations resulting from different spheres of their lives (McDonald 2000; Neyer et al. 2013).

Gender inequalities in Polish households are confirmed by the survey data. According to the ISSP in 2012 women with at least one child spend on average 23.4 h per week on household work (not including childcare and leisure time activities), whereas the equivalent figure for men is only 17.79 h. In comparison, childless women spent 20.14 h and childless men 15.58. These statistics show that for both men and women having children leads to an increase in time devoted to household work. Graph 5.1 shows these differences more clearly. Twenty-seven percent of childless men and 23% of fathers spent less than 5 h per week on household work, at the same time only 15% of childless women and 8% of mothers spend less than 5 h on such work. This shows that men more often withdraw from domestic duties. Yet it does not mean that these duties are not carried out—it rather means that they are transferred to women.

CBOS (Public Opinion Research Centre in Poland) conducts regular studies on the division of domestic work in Polish households. Even though men's participation in household duties has been increasing since 2004, by 2018 women were still mainly responsible for most of these duties (see Table 5.1). In over 80% of households, women usually do the laundry and ironing. Whereas in over 60% of households, women usually prepare meals and do the household cleaning. Men engage more often than women only in ordering external services and making minor repairs, which are not as engaging and time-consuming as other everyday domestic

5.1 Prevailing Inequalities in the Household

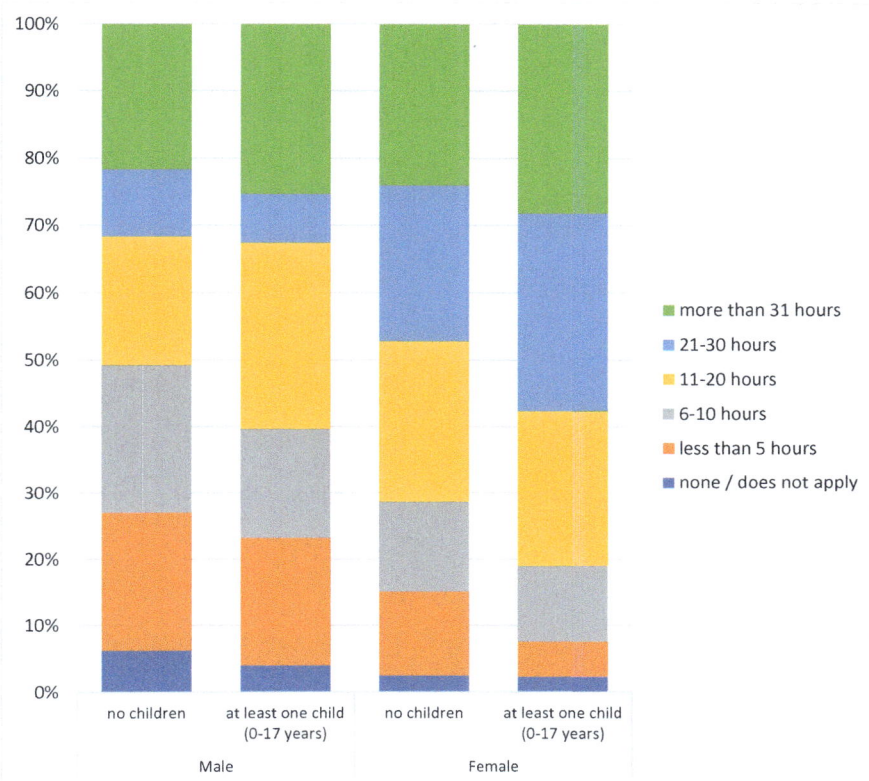

**Graph 5.1** On average, how many hours a week do you personally spend on household work, not including childcare and leisure time activities? Source ISSP 2012. Prepared by the author

duties. Thus even though in 2018 men were more involved in domestic work, gender inequality still persists.

Interestingly, the level of everyday practices is not congruent with what people have to say about sharing domestic duties. In the European Value Survey (EVS) in 2017 Poles were asked whether they thought that sharing household chores is important for a successful marriage or partnership. Only 5.5% of men and 3.8% of women said it is not very important. In general, women (51.7%) more often than men (47.7%) agreed that it is very important, but keeping in mind the low engagement of Polish men in domestic duties, the level of their agreement is still very high (see Graph 5.2).

Individuals' declarations and opinions are not always realised in practice. Maria Reimann (2019) in her research on Polish couples with an egalitarian approach to domestic and care duties shows that upon becoming parents they often lean to a more traditional model of the division of everyday obligations. Even though these couples declared that fairness and equality were important values for them, after having

**Table 5.1** Who in your household usually performs the following household duties?

|  | Men | | Women | | Jointly or N/A | |
| --- | --- | --- | --- | --- | --- | --- |
|  | 2004 | 2018 | 2004 | 2018 | 2004 | 2018 |
|  | Percentage | | | | | |
| Preparing meals | 6 | 5 | 76 | 65 | 18 | 30 |
| Washing dishes/loading and removing dishes from the dishwasher[a] | 8 | 13 | 71 | 56 | 21 | 31 |
| General cleaning | 6 | 4 | 69 | 61 | 25 | 35 |
| Thorough cleaning (window cleaning, rug beating) | 7 | 8 | 62 | 57 | 31 | 35 |
| Laundry | 3 | 2 | 87 | 82 | 10 | 15 |
| Ironing | 4 | 6 | 87 | 81 | 9 | 13 |
| Everyday shopping | 12 | 12 | 59 | 37 | 29 | 51 |
| Ordering external services | 66 | 60 | 19 | 17 | 25 | 23 |
| Making minor repairs |  | 81 |  | 7 |  | 12 |
| Taking out rubbish | 34 | 29 | 22 | 21 | 44 | 50 |

Source: CBOS 2018
[a]Added in 2018

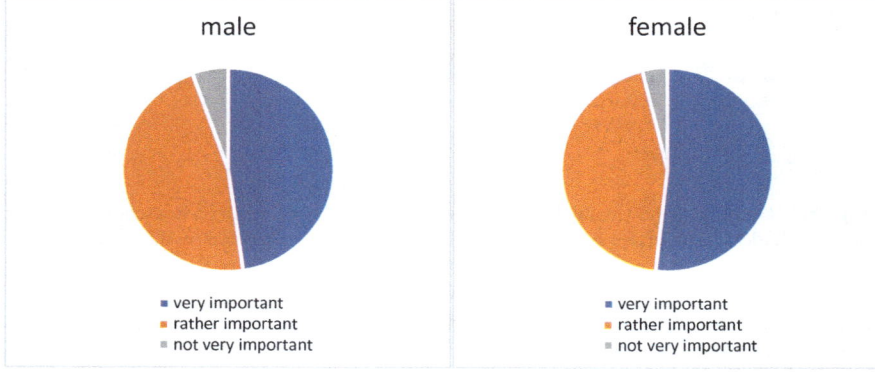

**Graph 5.2** Some people think that sharing household chores is important for a successful marriage or partnership. What do you think? Source EVS 2017. Prepared by the author

children women started to do more in the household. In such a way gendered beliefs were still present in their lives, but in a less explicit way. Similar conclusions are drawn by Magdalena Żadkowska (2016), who conducted research on the division of domestic work for Polish couples. She observes that there is a substantial change in a couple's life after childbirth—usually women undertake most domestic duties. They become mangers of everyday household obligations, whereas a man's job is to help her with these duties.

## 5.2 "I Try to Do as Much as I Can". Men and Domestic Chores

Analysis of in-depth interviews with Polish parents also indicates that there are significant differences in the engagement of men and women in domestic work. Even though the amount of time men spend on unpaid domestic work has increased in the twentieth century, they still spend fewer hours on domestic chores than women (Hook 2006). The interviewed couples can be divided into two types. The first type realises the model of a traditional family, in which women are mostly responsible for all the obligations in the household, whereas the role of men is not to interrupt or disturb women in their work.

> I: I guess I'd want him to ... how to say it ... not to do certain chores, but ... I mean if we have a second child, then it will be necessary, but now I'm fine. Although, I'd prefer him not to make a mess himself, oh! [laugh].
> R: You mean, he should not disturb you?
> I: Yes, yes. That's what I mean. [C18W25 Luiza]

In the second type, couples try to share domestic duties equally, they often discuss the division of obligations so as to ensure that the woman is not overwhelmed. One portion of such couples still struggle with an unequal or unfair share of the workload that is mostly experienced by women (more on the sense of fairness in Sect. 5.4). In both types, men's engagement in domestic work is often called 'help'. Perceiving men's domestic work in terms of *help* or *support* is characteristic for both mothers and fathers regardless of their working situation.

> The division [of domestic work] is fluid, I guess. [My wife] cooks, because I can't cook. So this situation evolved by itself. I try to help her in cleaning up, so she doesn't have to do it, yet it doesn't always work. [C4M5 Aleksander]

> We talked about it [the division of domestic work], but as I said, my husband is away all week, he comes back on Friday, so there's just Saturday and Sunday when he's tired because he travels a lot. So I got used to the fact that all these domestic duties are mine, although we do have fights about them because I'd like him to help me more. [C16W23 Ewelina]

The prevalence of using the word 'help', even by couples who have an equalitarian approach, suggests that men's role in the household is still perceived as secondary, and that men (but also women) do not fully internalise *new* norms resulting from the changing gender order. Some interviewed women, who are more aware of the prevailing gender inequalities and more reflexive about the organisation of everyday life, recognise the problem of using the word 'help' in the context of their partner's or husband's engagement in domestic work.

> I: So I like to cook, but you probably know how I feel, I like to cook on weekends, to prepare dinner for us in the evening, but not necessarily weekday cooking like sandwiches or a pork cutlet with potatoes. But my husband also cooks during weekdays. Not very complicated dishes, but he can cook something. Doing laundry, cooking, general cleaning we share all of that, but from the very beginning it always annoyed me, when he was saying that he would help me with something. This simply means that this is my thing but he can help out a bit.
> R: Yes, I can see how people would say that.

> I: Yes, men are *helpful* [original emphasis], so now I try to make him aware that these are our common responsibilities. [P1K1 Jola]

Jola's comment draws attention to the meaning hidden behind the word 'help'. Using such terms as 'help' or 'support' in the context of men's housework suggests that this work is not regarded as their main obligation even though they live in the same household and benefit from this work to the same extent as women (Jarska 2020). This also means that men have more power to choose what they do in the household. Interestingly, the interviewed men are perfectly aware that they do less than their partners or wives. I distinguish three main excuses they use to explain their lower engagement in domestic work. First, the interviews indicate that men often refer to traditional gender roles and a woman's predisposition to fulfil everyday domestic tasks.

> R: You're saying that your wife is sometimes angry that she does more than you. Are you trying to change it then?
> I: No, I think that I do more than an average man. But I know I do less than her, that's clear, but I think it's normal, we cannot expect this sudden change in a society that it [the division of domestic work] should be fifty-fifty now if it never was like that before. It's difficult to organise because I also think that women have a greater ability to combine different tasks. They have everything organised, they know how to handle stuff, whereas men don't have such a talent [laugh]. It's enough if they [men] sometimes do the dishes, vacuum or take the rubbish out or, I don't know, take care of children. [C5M6 Filip]

Filip's wife is perfectly aware of her husband's way of thinking and even though she does not agree with it, she accepts it.

> My husband assumes that a woman, me as a woman, as a more practical person can get more done [housework] and faster than him too. So he thinks that if I want something done quickly, then I should do it myself. [C5W7 Anna]

These division-based traditional gender roles are often reinforced by the division of paid work—when only the man is the sole breadwinner, then the woman stays at home (for example because of parental leave) and *naturally* undertake almost all domestic duties, even when she does not like it.

> I mean because my wife stays at home, she simply does more things. So laundry, cooking and other stuff is done by my wife. [C16M18 Bartosz]

> It's an ongoing battle. There's blood sometimes [laugh]. As I said, it's dynamic. At the beginning certain things meant my wife did all the housework, but she rebelled, and we argued a lot. On the one hand, she didn't work for pay, she was home a lot and I was working a lot, so practically all [household] obligations were on her shoulders. But she didn't like it. On the other hand, there was no other option. So we were both frustrated, me because I was tired after a full day at work, then had to hear complaints that I didn't help at home and that she worked hard but I didn't appreciate it. So now we're trying to deal with this. [C17M19 Mikołaj]

The second reason given for men's lower engagement in domestic work is connected to what Mikołaj mentioned in the above quote—men often indicate that they are too tired to participate in it more. This tiredness is usually a consequence of spending more hours on paid work than their partners or wives.

## 5.2 "I Try to Do as Much as I Can". Men and Domestic Chores

I: Sometimes I think I should do more about the house, but I don't have time.
R: Do you feel guilty?
I: Yes, yes. So I would like to do more, but if you come back from work tired, then you just want to rest. [C12M13 Darek]

In such a way the traditional division of paid work can reinforce the traditional division of domestic work. It is worth mentioning that even though men use the excuse of being tired the Time Use Survey conducted by Statistics Poland indicates that women in general spend more hours on 'duty time' than men (this includes paid work, voluntary work, domestic work, family work and education), whereas men have more rest time. This applies at each stage of life (Statistics Poland 2016). Thus the argument of long working hours used by the interviewed men usually refers only to hours spent on paid work but does not recognise work done in the household.

The third excuse made by men concerns the organisation of care work. The interviews indicate that many men avoid household duties by taking care of children.

I: One night I was wondering if we equally or unequally share [domestic and care duties] and how much time we spend with the kids. And I came to the conclusion that we share equally, but even though we share equally my wife does two thirds of the domestic work. This is because when I see a crisis, I leave.
R: What kind of crisis?
I: When there is a mess at home, such a big mess, then I run away. I just can't begin to . . .
R: But do you run away with the kids?
I: Yes, with the kids, I say we're going for a walk. No, I don't run away alone - no.[C2M3 Kamil]

He definitely is a super-dad, he spends lots of time with our son, but at some point it started to bother me, because I didn't have time to play with [my son], because I had too many things to do alone. And it ended up that I finished all the domestic duties but my son was so tired he went straight to sleep. [C4W5 Ela]

He spends lots of time with the kids. He more often reads to them, plays with them. And then I have time to deal with the domestic duties. [C5W7 Anna]

These findings are congruent with other research on fatherhood that indicates that men are responsible for the aspects of being a parent which are more fun—they are more often responsible for playing with children than for mundane everyday activities such as cooking or cleaning (Evertsson 2014; Johansson and Klinth 2008; Szlendak 2011). It can be assumed that this is because the reconstruction of masculinity models concentrates more on care practices than other traditional female obligations (Elliott 2016; Scambor et al. 2014). Men are relatively new actors in the area of domestic and care work, and so have greater power to choose what kind of activities they want to be involved in as fathers and members of the household. The activities they reject then have to be undertaken by women (Suwada 2017). Care work is often seen as more satisfying and valuable than domestic work (Bianchi et al. 2012; Sullivan 2013), so it is not surprising that men choose them over household duties. At the same time, men often recognise that their engagement in domestic work is lower than that of their partner or wife. For many of them it is a comfortable situation, even though they sometimes feel guilty about it.

## 5.3 "I Just Don't Want to Force Him". Women as Managers of Everyday Life

Men's approach to domestic work is strictly connected to the role of women in the domestic sphere. Unpaid work in the household is treated as a *natural* element of a woman's role in the family (Titkow et al. 2004). Consequently, even though women participate in the labour market, they are still expected to be responsible for work in the domestic sphere. Their partner or husband should support them in this work, yet this work is still seen as a woman's responsibility. Thus women are responsible for the smooth organisation of the household, they take the role of managers in domestic life. The narrative of Polish mothers indicates that they recognise their role as primary managers, and for many of them it is an overwhelming situation, which on the one hand often leads to arguments between partners, but on the other hand is perceived as unchangeable in each interviewee's current situation. According to the researched mothers, the inevitability of unequal division of domestic work results from different reasons. First, for many women being the domestic manger is to some extent comfortable, because they have control over everyday life.

> Sometimes I'd like to change something, but it's only when I'm really tired. In fact, I prefer doing everything my own way. Because, for example, when I see my husband vacuuming, I prefer to take this vacuum cleaner and do it by myself [laugh]. [C19W27 Róża]

> So I cook. When it comes to cleaning up, my husband tries to clean up, but he's generally slower, so sometimes I have to admit I don't want him to do it, even though he can do it, because I know I do it faster. I know that's a little bit crazy [laugh]. [C4W5 Ela]

Such an approach by women to domestic work can be interpreted as *gatekeeping*, a strategy which mothers often adopt to make sure her family is not at risk or does not miss some opportunities. In such a way women sustain their power within the family. The strategy of gatekeeping is more often than not used to describe women's approach to caregiving, yet it can also be adopted to depict a woman's managerial role in the context of allocating domestic work (Allen and Hawkins 1999; Gaunt 2007; Latshaw and Hale 2016). What is more, this narrative is often connected with reasoning based on personal preferences. In the interviews parents usually give an example of different definitions of cleanliness. Some people do not mind having a dirty kitchen or an unvacuumed carpet. For others such things are unbearable. Some interviewed parents refer to these differences to explain an unequal division of domestic work, yet the narratives indicate that women in general have higher standards of tidiness, and consequently, they more often end up doing more household duties, such as general cleaning, vacuuming or washing dishes.

> Everyone has a different standard learned at home of what tidiness means. And for me, for example, what is order for me is a mess for my wife. And for me vacuuming once a week is even too often but for her... she'd like to vacuum every day. So we're always going to fight about this. [C15M16 Witold]

## 5.3 "I Just Don't Want to Force Him". Women as Managers of Everyday Life

> Sometimes we'll have a minor quarrel about this [housework], but in general ... it's not like it's carved in stone that I have to do it, I don't feel it has to be me who does it, and nor does he. It's more that we feel we should get it done together. It's just that, well, sometimes my need to clean something up may be greater than his, and his need to rest at this time may be greater. [C2W3 Ola]

Yet it can be argued that personal preferences are shaped by socio-cultural structures. Women's greater focus on order in the household can be explained by gender beliefs, according to which a woman is expected to take care of domestic duties. These gender beliefs are learned in the process of socialisation (Chodorow 1999), which teaches boys and girls different attitudes to domestic chores. In such a way greater engagement in particular domestic duties is rather connected with prevailing models of masculinity and femininity than individual preferences. As the research of Natasza Kosakowska-Berezecka et al. (2018) indicates, some household activities are perceived as feminine, whereas others as masculine. Since activities connected to general cleaning and preparing meals are perceived as more feminine by Poles, the interviewed mothers and fathers can, sometimes even unconsciously, behave according to these perceptions, and consequently have a different approach to order and disorder in the household.

Mothers often compare themselves to others, in particular their own parents and other family members, to a time when the organisation of everyday life was even more traditional, to when men did not participate in domestic work at all. Many interviewed women emphasised that when they were children, their mothers were overwhelmed with domestic and care work, even though they usually worked for pay full-time, whereas their fathers did not know how to cook or clean and limited their parental obligations to breadwinning. In such a context when a partner or husband does *anything* in the household it is looked upon favourably.

> I think that in our family it isn't so bad [laugh]. I remember when I was a child there was a patriarchy. A husband was a king in his own castle, and a wife did all the work. For example, my mum did everything, managed all the family, did the cooking ... and she worked for pay even more than my father. That's just the way things were in those days. [C17W23 Irena]

These findings are congruent with the research of Theodore Greenstein (2009) on household labour, in which he found that satisfaction with the fairness of dividing household labour is moderated by the level of gender equity in the national context. This means that women compare their situation to that of others, and are either more satisfied/dissatisfied with the division of household duties in their family. My study suggests that they not only make a comparison with women in a similar situation, but also to previous generations.

A recurring theme in the interviews with mothers is the need to force men to engage in more domestic duties. Women often have to constantly remind their partner or husband that they need to wash the dishes, vacuum, clean the bathroom and so on. Many such women are actually tired of this constant reminding and consequently prefer to do it themselves.

> I sometimes feel bad that I nag him and say "Hey, you need to clean up" or "Do this and do that" [grimace], you know? I don't like ... I don't like myself in such a role. But on the other

hand, if I don't remind him, it doesn't get done. And this is a perennial problem [...]. Why can't he clean up of his own free will? Why? [C2W3 Ola]

It's a nightmare to force him to do anything. I need to remind him. I talked to my girlfriends and they say it's the same for them too. That you need to remind him, sometimes even a few times, that he needs to do something. [C5W7 Anna]

He's more involved [in domestic work] when I yell at him. But it's only for five minutes. It's getting better - he is trying. I know he works and he's tired. But on the other hand I'm tired too with this monotony of constantly being with the children and with the lack of time for myself. It's very difficult. [C16W23 Ewelina]

These narratives indicate that Polish mothers, overwhelmed with duties resulting from paid work, care work and domestic work, are also responsible for making their male partners more involved in household work. Somehow they become responsible for their husband sharing domestic duties with them—in a way they are responsible for introducing a partnership into their relationship.

## 5.4 "I Think It's Fair". The Sense of Fairness and Gender Roles

According to the 2012 ISSP data 59% of women with children aged 0–17 years think that they do more than their fair share. Less than 3% think that they do less than their fair share. At the same time 36.6% of men with children aged 0–17 admit that they do less than their fair share, while 55.4% declare that they do roughly their fair share (see Graph 5.3).

This data shows that there is a discrepancy in how people perceive the division of domestic duties in the household, whether they consider it fair or unfair. A sense of fairness is very subjective and each partner in a couple may assess the division differently. Thus as interviews with Polish parents indicate, discussions about this issue are often challenging and lead to misunderstandings. This issue is especially difficult for women, who do not always have the ability or strength to explain their point of view. They sometimes lack the external, objective measures which help them to prove their stance.

I mean talking about this ... I mean sometimes I dream of having a neutral observer, someone who could record my day, because I simply don't have time to do it. And at the end of each day this observer could tell [my partner] "Listen, her day looked like this: from the early morning she did this, that and the other. I'm not being funny, but it's simply too much for her, it's unfair". I can't tell him this, I don't know how to do it. It's very difficult for me, so I need a witness ... this remains unsaid, all this grief and anger which is cumulating every day. It's so hard for me, emotionally hard. [C3W4 Joanna]

The issue of fairness appeared very often in the interviews with Polish parents in the context of domestic work. Yet it should be noted here that the concept of fairness does not have to imply equal division of domestic work. As Jonathan Ives notes, fairness 'is highly subjective and context dependent, and supervenes on facts such as

## 5.4 "I Think It's Fair". The Sense of Fairness and Gender Roles

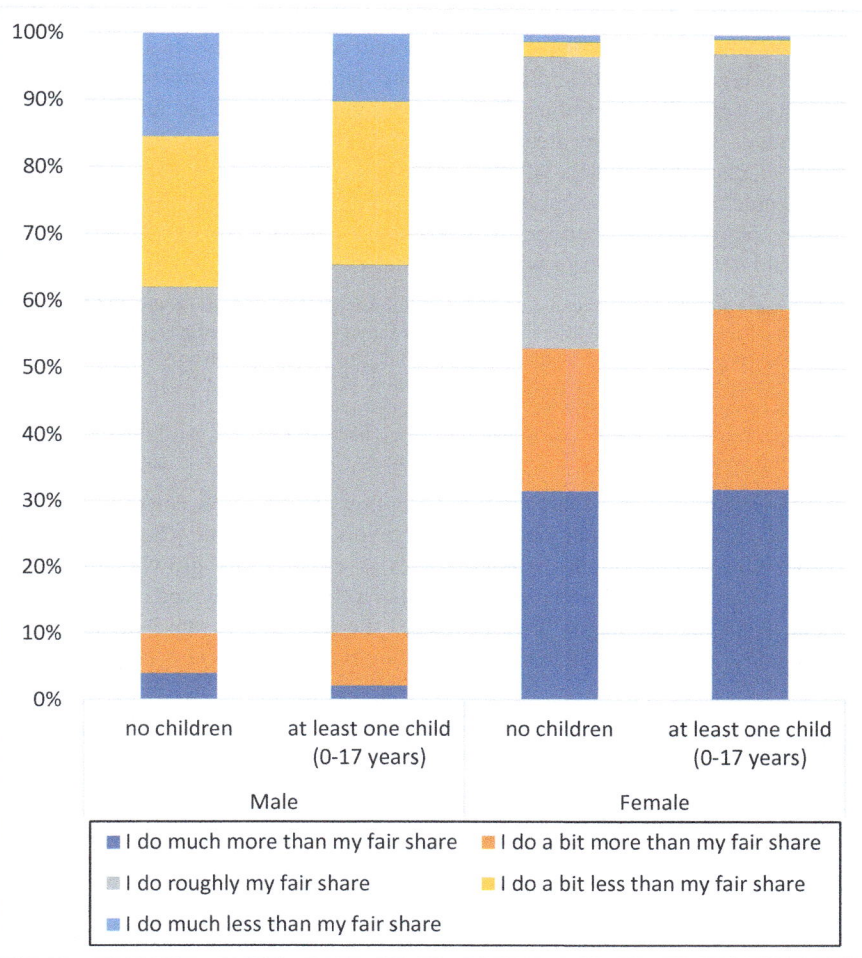

**Graph 5.3** Which of the following best applies to the sharing of household work between you and your spouse/partner? Source ISSP 2012. Prepared by the author

expectations, relationship norms, appetite for certain kinds of work, capacity and competence. Therefore, what is fair in the context of one couple will not be fair in another, and what is considered *fair* overall may not be what is *equal*' (Ives 2015, p. 289). Thus the issue of fairness is not about objective justice, but rather a type of social contract on the domestic level (Olcoń-Kubicka 2020). Different conceptions of fairness were visible in the interviews with Polish parents. Fairness does not have to mean that the opportunity structures for mothers and the fathers are exactly the same, but rather that they perceive their situation as fair and acceptable. It is also important that both parents agree on the organisation of work and everyday life.

Following Jonathan Ives' study (2015) on how fathers construct fairness in their fathering practices, I distinguish three different ways fairness is defined in the context of household duties. First, there are parents who perceive fairness as reciprocity. This way of thinking refers to a traditional model of family in which the mother is the primary carer and the father is the primary breadwinner. Yet because of changing models of masculinity and femininity these roles are not unchangeable, and there is a need for each person in the relationship to recognise the burden placed on their partner. In my Polish interviews it is usually stressed that a man should *help* his partner or wife with domestic duties.

> I: You know it's changing, because when [my wife] was working this division was different, when she stays at home, it's different. So it's now rather rigid, but it changes sometimes. So from the very beginning ... at the very beginning [my wife] was already pregnant [and stayed at home] and she has always been doing more of the domestic duties.
> R: So do you think it's fair? Would you change anything?
> I: I guess I'm more content with it than [my wife], because I do less, but I think it's fair. [C16M16 Witold]

Yet the interviews show that such a perception of fairness is not very common, and is rarely accepted by both partners. It only works for a couple when both parents hold the same view, and this often changes as children are growing up. In the following citation Irena says that even though as a couple they agreed on a traditional division at the beginning of their marriage, she still had a sense of unfairness. Consequently, at the time of the interview they were trying a new organisation of work.

> And even though he helped me, I had this feeling of asymmetry, because for me the time spent on care and domestic work seemed endless, you know, but time spent on paid work is limited. He had free time, but I had a feeling I never had free time [...]. But I wasn't sure if I could make any demands, because whenever we started to argue, he'd say: "But this is what we agreed on – I work, you take care of the home." I just didn't feel comfortable with this situation. [C17W23 Irena]

The considerations of Irena are congruent with a second way of defining fairness—fairness as equality. Parents who perceive fairness in terms of equality try to divide time spent on domestic duties equally or try to share all tasks (see also: Reimann 2016). This usually requires some discussion by the couple (usually initiated by the woman) and careful calculation on how much time each task takes.

> R: Did you discuss this division [that the woman cooks, the man cleans up]? Or did it just happen?
> I: No, no. It was hard work. One day I noted how many hours each duty takes, and I showed it to [my partner]. How much time it takes to cook each day, do the shopping and so on. [My partner] also cooks, but rarely, occasionally. It's rather a matter of choice than necessity, you know? So when he feels like it, he cooks something [...]. So I showed him how many hours all these different tasks take, and told him that I would rather not clean the toilet, so that we need to set the division [of labour]. In short – we set the division.
> R: Ok. So do you now have a sense of fair division?
> I: No, I cook more, much more than he cleans up in terms of time. [C10W12 Weronika]

## 5.4 "I Think It's Fair". The Sense of Fairness and Gender Roles

This approach is very difficult to maintain because it requires calculations and sticking to an arranged division of work. That is why many parents, who perceive fairness as equality, talk about it in terms of *trying* rather than an actual situation. Fairness as equality is not something that is easily achieved, but something which people aim for. What is more, parents sometimes experience trouble when demarking boundaries between different types of work. In the strategy of fairness as equality it is important not to confuse time spent on paid work or care work with time spent on domestic work, because then there is a risk of ending up in a relationship based on traditional gender roles, which is something that such parents try to avoid.

> I was thinking several times about it [a fair division of domestic duties] and it's very difficult, especially in such a relationship as ours in which I work full-time and [my wife] has a nonstandard schedule. [But] you need to do your paid work duties and then domestic duties [...] you should not compensate for the fact that you work more by avoiding domestic duties. [C7M8 Stefan]

Finally, fairness is perceived in terms of functional specialisations. It is based on the assumption that people are good in different things, and so they split their responsibilities along those lines. Such an approach is often connected with personal preferences, in particular it helps to avoid those obligations which are particularly disliked by one person in a couple. Yet it is important that this division applies only to domestic duties and there is no confusion of time devoted to paid work with that of domestic/care work.

> I: With this division it's like – who likes what. I hate taking the rubbish out, so I don't do it at all. I don't like washing the dishes either. I have traumatic memories from childhood, when I was forced to do the dishes. So we try to do different things. I was interested in child feeding, so I do that. It's not always perfect, but it works somehow.
> R: So do you have a sense of fairness?
> I: I have a sense that we're trying. I have a feeling that we're both overloaded [laugh]. We're both tired and as my friend said: "I'd like him to do more, but when I think about it, I know he doesn't have time for it." [C11W13 Sylwia]
>
> R: So do you feel that your organisation of domestic work is fair?
> I: Yes. I don't expect [my husband] to do 50% because he does a lot. And I know that I do more in some areas and that's ok because there are lots of things he does which he's good at. [C8W10 Iga]

Analysis of the interviews shows that household work creates the most quarrels and misunderstandings between couples. Domestic duties are perceived as the most boring, continuous and often senseless, since their effects do not last long. What is more, this kind of work is the most undervalued, and individuals performing most of such tasks feel that their hard work is not recognised as important. This might have negative consequences for the relationship. Hence the narratives of parents indicate that there is a great effort to make this division fair in different ways.

## 5.5 "We Have a Lady Coming Once a Week". Strategies to Reduce Domestic Duties

Keeping in mind the problem of fairness in the division of domestic work, it is not surprising that many parents develop different strategies to reduce the amount of time spent on it. One strategy, adopted by more affluent parents, is to outsource domestic work by hiring household help. This is one of the most effective ways of reducing conflicts over the division of domestic work and relieving mothers.

> We don't have any conflicts about domestic chores, but that's because there is this lady who comes once a week and neatly cleans the apartment [...]. We have our aunt Marta, a lady who comes to clean up. And she cleans up the apartment and does the ironing. So fortunately, we don't have to do it. There is an informal division that I'm responsible for laundry and my husband for dishes and the dishwasher. [C6W8 Ida]

> We hire Mrs. Maria, she comes once a week and cleans up, it's simply wonderful! [C3W4 Joanna]

Yet for many parents such a solution is too expansive, they cannot afford to hire anyone to help with household chores. Many parents also recognise the importance of household appliances that help to avoid some tiring and troublesome duties such as washing clothes or dishes and assist in many household obligations.

> I: We don't have much trouble. We have a dishwasher, so there is no problem with this [dirty dishes].
> R: So I guess you have no problems with laundry either?
> I: No, no problem. And we've changed the washing machine to a washer-dryer, so now we don't have to hang clothes up to dry. You put the clothes in, they are washed, dried and you just take them out. Voila! [...] All this stuff is automatised. Thirty years ago my parents didn't have such conveniences. [C6M7 Krzysztof]

> I: In the new house we plan to have a dishwasher. It's the most important item because sometimes I get the impression that I spend all day Sunday washing dishes, and I don't know how it happens, where do they all come from? [...] Besides, I want this automated vacuum cleaner and mop, but [my husband] is not convinced...
> R: Automated mop?
> I: Yes, one is vacuuming and the other is cleaning the floor, they communicate with each other, and they do it all when you're not at home. So you go out, they clean, and when you come back everything is done. It's so cool! [C2W3 Ola]

Other sources of help are often the children's grandmothers, who sometimes engage in domestic duties when visiting their grandchildren.

> Sometimes, once or twice a month my mum comes to look after the kid, then she does the dishes, cleans the kitchen or, I don't know, tidies up in the living room. And when my mother-in-law visits, she does the ironing or cooks. But it's not that often. (C17W23 Irena)

The help of grandparents, in particular grandmothers, is especially visible with single parents, who are solely responsible for all domestic duties.

> When I lived with my husband, we had a household helper, but now I don't. I mean my mum comes often, more often than before [...]. She comes willingly, without any fights then stays

## 5.5 "We Have a Lady Coming Once a Week". Strategies to Reduce Domestic Duties

for two or three days and deals with the household. She cooks something and helps with the children in the morning. It's a great help. [S2W2 Ewa]

R: And when it comes to household chores, since you live with your parents now, how does it work?
I: I definitely have seventy percent less than before. You know I like cooking. I like it very much [...] so before [the divorce and move back to her parents] I never thought about it as something, I don't know, scary. It was normal, you have to eat breakfast, dinner and supper, but of course there were days when I was tired, but ... now when I'm tired my mum always cooks something. There is always something to eat now. [S4W14 Agata]

The help of grandmothers is especially appreciated by single parents, who often experience a greater burden of domestic work than parents in couples. This is notably evident in the case of single fathers, who after splitting up with their partner need to undertake all domestic duties that they did not carry out before.

Definitely, I have more now. In a sense that in fact, before, we had a rather conservative model and most duties were done by my wife, like cleaning up and cooking, it [the division of labour] was like eighty percent to twenty percent. And now I deal with all these household duties on my own. Sometimes someone helps me, but it's very rare. So I see changes and feel them, my ex-wife also as I still talk to her. It's much more difficult to deal with everything. [S1M2 Marek]

All these everyday things like shopping, laundry and everything I have to do alone, alone. Everyone laughs that I have muscular arms and asks if I'm working out or something, and I say "shopping bags and climbing stairs" [laugh]. So I laugh, but yeah ... I have no choice. Nobody else does it for me. [S3W6 Iwona]

Possibility structures which reduce the hours spent on domestic duties vary greatly. Most of all, there is a difference between parents according to economic resources. More affluent parents can more easily afford to hire domestic help, and thereby save time for themselves and their family. For less affluent parents the situation depends on the availability of grandparents, mostly grandmothers, who can come and help. But it should be noted that grandparents are not always willing to help, quite often they live too far away to be able to provide support. Thus some parents adopt coping strategies: not performing less urgent duties or postponing them. Single parents, who have such a possibility, usually do such duties when their children spend time with the second parent.

The only time I have to relax is when my ex-husband takes the children every other weekend, [...]. And to be honest, one weekend a fortnight is enough for me to regenerate. And this is also the time to thoroughly clean the flat, I don't know, mop the floor, wash the bathroom, do some big shopping. So it's not only for me, but also for the flat. [S2W2 Ewa]

Other parents deal with the lack of time by doing domestic duties in the so called 'meantime'. The strategy of meantime is especially available for parents who can do at least part of their paid work from home. This is the case for Weronika, who can cook in between different working tasks.

R: Why are you responsible for cooking?
I: Because I can do it in the meantime. And I prefer cooking to cleaning. [C10W12 Weronika]

But it is also a common strategy for parents who are responsible for looking after their children.

> You often long for a day when you can get something [household work] done in the meantime. But sometimes it's impossible [...]. So when you're staying home and have nothing to do and your child falls asleep, then you can tidy up, can't you? [C2W3 Ola]

All these strategies show that even though domestic work is not given much importance, and is often perceived as a burden, it still has to be done. Domestic work, even though often invisible and unrecognised, is an important element of individuals' everyday life so cannot be omitted.

## 5.6 Conclusion

The interviewed parents perceive domestic work as the least important of all types of work done in connection with parenthood. It is the most boring and is perceived as never ending, since their efforts are not long-lasting (Oakley 2018). Domestic duties are also the area of greatest conflict for couples. Parents argue less often over the division of paid work and care work, this is because these types of work are recognised as important and (can) bring satisfaction. Similarly, as is the case for paid work and care work, domestic work is a highly gendered area of social life. Yet the interviews of the Polish mothers indicate that for them the gendered division of domestic work is particularly painful and least understood. Women perform more domestic duties than men in general. As Latshaw and Hale's study indicates (2016), even in families with breadwinning mothers and stay-at-home fathers, women undertake domestic and care duties when they are at home (during evenings, weekends and holidays), instead of having leisure time. According to Latshaw and Hale (2016), stay-at-home fathers enjoy substantially greater amounts of leisure time than breadwinning mothers, stay-at-home mothers, or employed fathers who work full-time or part-time. Gender beliefs impose on women an obligation to be the person who is mainly responsible for the household, regardless of their other duties. That is why in times of changing gender roles mothers are managers of the everyday functioning of the household, whereas men are perceived as helpers who provide support when needed. At the same time, such gender relations are hard to explain by biological differences alone. In Chap. 3 on care work, I argued that parents often refer to biological differences to explain the difference of engagement in care work for men and women. The main argument was based on a woman's ability to breastfeed—men as the ones who lack such an ability were excluded from many caregiving practices. Even though such reasoning is not sound for every interviewed parent, for many of them it is logical and can explain the differences between the level of engagement in care work between men and women. Domestic work cannot be explained in the same way. There are no biological differences between men and women which would justify women spending more time on household duties than men. It is rather a matter of prevailing gender beliefs which are social and cultural constructs grounded in the structures of social inequalities. Consequently, Polish mothers who work full-time and are perceived as the main caregivers, are overwhelmed with domestic duties which they expect to be shared more equally with their husbands or partners. Interestingly, when asked even men agree that in general sharing domestic duties is important for a successful marriage or partnership.

Analysis of the interviews indicates that parents adopt different definitions of fairness. Fairness does not have to mean equal time spent on domestic duties, but is rather connected with an agreement between the couple, it corresponds with other parental obligations resulting from paid and care work. Similarly, as in the case of the organisation of care work, it is important to recognise the differences resulting from economic resources as well as from the specific family situation. It is easier for more affluent parents to outsource household duties to external help. Some parents can count on help from grandmothers. In both of these cases the gender inequalities are particularly visible. Household duties are transferred from mothers to other women—a female household helper or a grandmother. Such strategies, even though they help with fulfilling parental obligations, reinforce gender inequalities. They do not change men's approach to domestic duties, but rather can strengthen beliefs that such duties are feminine.

# References

Allen, S. M., & Hawkins, A. J. (1999). Maternal gatekeeping: Mothers' beliefs and behaviors that inhibit greater father involvement in family work. *Journal of Marriage and Family, 61*(1), 199–212. https://doi.org/10.2307/353894.

Bianchi, S. M., Sayer, L. C., Milkie, M. A., & Robinson, J. P. (2012). Housework: Who did, does or will do it, and how much does it matter? *Social Forces, 91*(1), 55–63. https://doi.org/10.1093/sf/sos120.

Bird, C. E., & Ross, C. E. (1993). Houseworkers and paid workers: Qualities of the work and effects on personal control. *Journal of Marriage and Family, 55*(4), 913–925. JSTOR. https://doi.org/10.2307/352772.

Chodorow, N. (1999). *The reproduction of mothering: Psychoanalysis and the sociology of gender: With a new preface*. University of California Press.

Coltrane, S. (2000). Research on household labor: Modeling and measuring the social embeddedness of routine family work. *Journal of Marriage and Family, 62*(4), 1208–1233. https://doi.org/10.1111/j.1741-3737.2000.01208.x.

Elliott, K. (2016). Caring masculinities theorizing an emerging concept. *Men and Masculinities, 19*(3), 240–259. https://doi.org/10.1177/1097184X15576203.

Evertsson, M. (2014). Gender ideology and the sharing of housework and child care in Sweden. *Journal of Family Issues, 35*(7), 927–949. https://doi.org/10.1177/0192513X14522239.

Fuwa, M. (2004). Macro-level gender inequality and the division of household labor in 22 countries. *American Sociological Review, 69*(6), 751–767. https://doi.org/10.1177/000312240406900601.

Gaunt, R. (2007). Maternal gatekeeping: Antecedents and consequences. *Journal of Family Issues, 29*(3), 373–395. https://doi.org/10.1177/0192513X07307851.

Greenstein, T. N. (2009). National context, family satisfaction, and fairness in the division of household labor. *Journal of Marriage and Family, 71*(4), 1039–1051. https://doi.org/10.1111/j.1741-3737.2009.00651.x.

Hochschild, A., & Machung, A. (2003). *The second shift*. Penguin Books.

Hook, J. L. (2006). Care in context: Men's unpaid work in 20 countries, 1965–2003. *American Sociological Review, 71*(4), 639–660. https://doi.org/10.1177/000312240607100406.

Ives, J. (2015). Theorising the 'deliberative father': Compromise, progress and striving to do fatherhood well. *Families, Relationships and Societies, 4*(2), 281–294. https://doi.org/10.1332/204674314X14184029517584.

Jarska, N. (2020). Men as husbands and fathers in postwar Poland (1956-1975): Towards new masculine identities? *Men and Masculinities*. https://doi.org/10.1177/1097184X20910492.

Johansson, T., & Klinth, R. (2008). Caring fathers the ideology of gender equality and masculine positions. *Men and Masculinities, 11*(1), 42–62. https://doi.org/10.1177/1097184X06291899.

Kosakowska-Berezecka, N., Jurek, P., Besta, T., Korzeniewska, L., & Seibt, B. (2018). De-gender them! Gendered vs cooperative division of housework – cross-cultural comparison of Polish and Norwegian students. *Current Psychology*. https://doi.org/10.1007/s12144-018-9915-6.

Kuhhirt, M. (2012). Childbirth and the long-term division of labour within couples: How do substitution, bargaining power, and norms affect parents' time allocation in West Germany? *European Sociological Review, 28*(5), 565–582. https://doi.org/10.1093/esr/jcr026.

Latshaw, B. A., & Hale, S. I. (2016). 'The domestic handoff': Stay-at-home fathers' time-use in female breadwinner families. *Journal of Family Studies, 22*(2), 97–120. https://doi.org/10.1080/13229400.2015.1034157.

McDonald, P. (2000). Gender equity in theories of fertility transition. *Population and Development Review, 26*(3), 427–439. https://doi.org/10.1111/j.1728-4457.2000.00427.x.

Neyer, G., Lappegård, T., & Vignoli, D. (2013). Gender equality and fertility: Which equality matters? *European Journal of Population/Revue Européenne de Démographie, 29*(3), 245–272. https://doi.org/10.1007/s10680-013-9292-7.

Oakley, A. (2018). *The sociology of housework (reissue)*. Policy Press.

Olcoń-Kubicka, M. (2020). Pursuit of fairness in household financial arrangements among young middle-class couples in Poland. *Journal of Consumer Culture, 20*(2), 156–174. https://doi.org/10.1177/1469540519891272.

Reimann, M. (2016). Searching for egalitarian divisions of care: Polish couples at the life-course transition to parenthood. In D. Grunow & M. Evertsson (Eds.), *Couples' transitions to parenthood: Analysing gender and work in Europe* (pp. 221–242). Edward Elgar Publishing.

Reimann, M. (2019). It is not something we consciously do: Polish couples struggles to maintain gender equality after the birth of their first child. In D. Grunow & M. Evertsson (Eds.), *New parents in Europe. Work-care practices, gender norms and family policies* (pp. 188–206). Edward Elgar Publishing.

Scambor, E., Bergmann, N., Wojnicka, K., Belghiti-Mahut, S., Hearn, J., Holter, Ø. G., et al. (2014). Men and gender equality: European insights. *Men and Masculinities, 17*(5), 552–577. https://doi.org/10.1177/1097184X14558239.

Schober, P. S. (2013). The parenthood effect on gender inequality: Explaining the change in paid and domestic work when British couples become parents. *European Sociological Review, 29*(1), 74–85. https://doi.org/10.1093/esr/jcr041.

Sirianni, C., & Negrey, C. (2000). Working time as gendered time. *Feminist Economics, 6*(1), 59–76. https://doi.org/10.1080/135457000337679.

Solera, C., & Mencarini, L. (2018). The gender division of housework after the first child: A comparison among Bulgaria, France and the Netherlands. *Community, Work & Family, 21*(5), 519–540. https://doi.org/10.1080/13668803.2018.1528969.

Statistics Poland. (2016). Budżet czasu ludności 2013. Część II [Time use survey 2013. Part 2].

Sullivan, O. (2013). What do we learn about gender by analyzing housework separately from child care? Some considerations from time-use evidence. *Journal of Family Theory & Review, 5*(2), 72–84. https://doi.org/10.1111/jftr.12007.

Suwada, K. (2017). *Men, fathering and the gender trap. Sweden and Poland compared*. Palgrave Macmillan.

Szlendak, T. (2011). *Socjologia rodziny: Ewolucja, historia, zróżnicowanie*. Wydawnictwo Naukowe PWN.

# References

Taniguchi, H., & Kaufman, G. (2020). Sharing the load: Housework, joint decision-making, and marital quality in Japan. *Journal of Family Studies*, 1–20. https://doi.org/10.1080/13229400.2020.1769707.

Titkow, A., Duch-Krzystoszek, D., & Budrowska, B. (2004). *Nieodpłatna praca kobiet: Mity, realia, perspektywy*. Wydawnictwo IFiS PAN.

Żadkowska, M. (2016). *Para w praniu: Codzienność, partnerstwo, obowiązki domowe*. Wydawnictwo Uniwersytetu Gdańskiego.

**Open Access** This chapter is licensed under the terms of the Creative Commons Attribution 4.0 International License (http://creativecommons.org/licenses/by/4.0/), which permits use, sharing, adaptation, distribution and reproduction in any medium or format, as long as you give appropriate credit to the original author(s) and the source, provide a link to the Creative Commons license and indicate if changes were made.

The images or other third party material in this chapter are included in the chapter's Creative Commons license, unless indicated otherwise in a credit line to the material. If material is not included in the chapter's Creative Commons license and your intended use is not permitted by statutory regulation or exceeds the permitted use, you will need to obtain permission directly from the copyright holder.

# Chapter 6
# Conclusions: Parenting in Times of Prevailing Inequalities

**Abstract** The final chapter of the book briefly summarises the key points of the previous chapters and addresses the central conclusions of the book. I underline how analysing parenting from the perspective of three types of work (paid work, care work and domestic work) help to recognise prevailing gender and economic inequalities in Polish society. I also argue that the opportunity structures of mothers and fathers greatly differ, and that it has its sources in the family policy system.

**Keywords** Paid work · Care work · Domestic work · Gender inequalities · Poland · Power relations

## 6.1 Parenting Work

Parenting is one of the most common experiences people have. Many of us are parents, some of us are planning on becoming parents, all of us have parents (even if we do not know them personally). In this context, it is not surprising that parenthood is a phenomenon often researched in social sciences, in particular in the sociology of families. At the same time, the common experience of people living in neoliberal societies is the experience of paid work. To satisfy basic human needs individuals need to have money that can be earned in the labour market. As I argued in Chap. 4, paid work is a crucial aspect of life. Today almost every adult person is expected to engage in paid work. These two elements of social life in contemporary times—parenthood and paid work—are crucial for studies of family life. Social scientists, as well as policy-makers, often refer to the concept of the work/life balance, the aim of which is to recognise that an individual has various roles in life and that they need to combine obligations arising from these roles (Drobnič 2011). Such an approach can be particularly useful in organisational studies to analyse how employees combine their various family obligations with those arising from paid work (Bozionelos and Hughes 2007; Nordenmark 2002). It can also be helpful for social policy, especially in times of decreasing fertility rates and policy-makers' aims to support parents in providing care for their children (Blofield and Martinez Franzoni 2015; Caracciolo di Torella and Masselot 2010). Yet as I argue, the concept of a work/life balance is not very useful from a sociological perspective since it does not allow for a critical description of contemporary social reality but it rather promotes one acceptable way of living that is based on a combination of parenthood on the one hand and engagement in paid work in the labour market on the other. What is more, this concept also assumes that there is a clear boundary between parenthood and paid work, between paid work activities and other activities in which an individual engages in everyday life. The experiences of Polish parents indicate that there is not such a clear boundary.

Thus in this book I proposed to look at the experience of parenthood from the perspective of three types of work: care work, paid work and domestic work. I claim here, following the reasoning of Oriel Sullivan (2013), who proposed analysing housework separately from child care, that distinguishing these three types of work helps to understand prevailing gender inequalities and can have implications for gender, family and labour market policies. The analysis presented in the previous chapters shows that in Polish society at the beginning of the twenty-first century there are still considerable gender inequalities. In the case of care work, women are still perceived as the main caregivers. This role is reinforced with the process of naturalisation, in which women are perceived at *natural caregivers* because of their biological abilities to become pregnant and to breastfeed (Suwada 2015, 2017). These initial biological differences have great consequences on how care work is organised in the household—who takes parental leave and who withdraws from paid work when there is a lack of institutional care for the children. This also puts stronger pressure on women who are active in the labour market. Economic resources can help in reducing this pressure by creating greater opportunity structures for the organisation of care work. Yet still, regardless of the economic situation of the family, women are perceived as the main caregivers. The inequalities in the organisation of care work are connected with inequalities in the area of paid work. Men's participation in the labour market is unquestioned. The role of the father is still recognised mostly in terms of economic provision. Fathers have to work for pay, regardless of their job satisfaction or working conditions. Paid work in their case is a crucial parenting obligation. The paid work of women, even though acceptable and for many families even necessary, is rather seen in terms of a secondary activity resulting from economic pressures and a woman's personal need to develop. It is more acceptable for mothers to resign from paid work when that work is unsatisfactory or too time-consuming and hinders care and domestic obligations. In the third type of work—household chores—gender inequalities are also palpable. In contrast to care work and paid work such inequalities are at least acceptable to Polish parents, especially mothers. Women are overwhelmed with domestic duties. Each week they spend more time on them than men, they also have to be everyday managers who force men to be more active in the domestic sphere. A man's role is perceived in terms of help or support, and consequently they have a greater ability to choose their level of engagement in domestic duties. Similarly, as is the case for care work, economic resources significantly expand opportunity structures of parents, who can more easily outsource domestic obligations to others. In all these types of work the situation of single parents is distinctly different. They do not have another person with whom they could share different parental obligations. They more acutely experience lack of time and insufficient support from the welfare state.

As I have claimed in the previous chapters, it might sometimes be difficult to find clear boundaries between these three types of work. Especially in the case of men, but this also applies to women, it is clear that paid work can be defined as one way of performing care work. The interviewed parents noticed that their approach to paid work changes in connection to parenthood. They feel a greater pressure that they need to work for pay, they also need to look more carefully at their level of earnings. Having children costs money, and as a responsible parent, they have to earn enough money to fulfil the needs of their children. In this context, paid work should not be understood as an obstacle to parental obligations, but rather as one of the most important parental duties. Paid work can be seen as one type of care work. Similarly, there is no clear boundary between care work and domestic work. As many studies show, becoming a parent results in an increase of domestic duties. Many of these chores are an element of taking care of children—preparing meals, shopping, cleaning the house, doing laundry, ironing and so on. In my opinion, this lack of clear boundaries between these different types of work may indicate that care work is the most important aspect of parenthood. Care work lies at the heart of parenting. As a result of having children mothers and fathers change their attitude to paid work and domestic work, as well as their everyday practices resulting from paid work and domestic work. Taking care of children, especially when they are small, becomes a central task in their everyday life that determines the organisation of all work.

## 6.2 Opportunity Structures of Polish Parents and Prevailing Inequalities

The way people realise their parental obligations is not only a result of their personal preferences. In this book I have referred to the theoretical perspective of agency that tries to understand the links between individual practices with societal structures on a macro level. People take actions in a particular social context, these actions are limited by constraints. Social action is an outcome of a choice made within constraints. Therefore, I have used the concept of opportunity structures to describe the situation of Polish parents within which they have to realise their parental obligations. Thanks to analysis through the triple lens of three different types of work, it becomes evident that different parents are characterised by different opportunity structures. I have argued that in-depth interviews, on which this work is based, allowed Polish parents to reflexively assess their situations, their opportunity structures, and to depict the actions they undertake in everyday life. Parents often indicated the limits that constrained the choices they could make in connection to fulfilling parental obligations. Such an approach enables a critical assessment of parenting in Polish society from the perspective of gender and economic inequalities.

Let us look first at the opportunity structures of men and women. The analysis presented in this book has shown that they differ significantly. In contemporary parenting practices individuals refer to traditional gender roles which affect the way men and women engage in different types of work. As Jennifer Hook notes: 'Women's responsibility for the home limits employment and advancement, and men's responsibility for breadwinning limits relationships with children' (Hook 2010, p. 1481). Even so, women's participation in the labour market is acceptable in Polish society, it is clear that as a society we did not get to the second phase of gender revolution, in which the importance of men's participation in the domestic sphere is recognised. In the literature there is plenty of research indicating the emergence of the new model of involved fatherhood (Doucet 2004; Dowd 2000; Wall and Arnold 2007). This is often perceived as a result of the changing gender order and changing models of masculinity. According to the theory of caring masculinities (Elliott 2016; Hanlon 2012; Scambor et al. 2014), men's engagement in care work is a crucial step towards a society based on gender equality. One way to achieve this is for fathers to be more involved in care work. Yet my analysis indicates that even though there is a big group of men who are actively engaged in care work, they still have greater power than women to choose the exact nature of this involvement. For example, I showed in Chap. 5 how men use a strategy of avoiding domestic work by taking care of children. In such a way gender inequalities prevail in a more nuanced way, they are subtly woven into everyday life.

The category of choice is crucial to understand the power relations prevailing in the household. Based on the narratives of the interviewed parents, I distinguished four types of a right of choice that parents can have. These are: (1) a right of choice to engage in satisfactory paid work, (2) a right of choice to go on parental leave, (3) a right to choose how to organise care work, and (4) a right to choose the level of engagement in domestic work. In a way these four rights create the opportunity structures of different parents. If we take into consideration the dimension of gender, as with economic resources and the family situation, it is clear that the opportunity structures of different parents vary. To understand how these rights of choice are exercised, it is important to distinguish two types of power an individual has in a couple—*situational power* and *debilitative power*. Using these two types of power I refer to the research of Caroline Gatrell (2007), who utilised the concepts from Carol Smart and Bren Neale (1998). Gatrell researched 'how fathers challenged [a] mother's sphere of influence by asserting their parental "rights" *within* marriage/co-habitation' (Gatrell 2007, p. 353). Situational power is based on resources, and so is easy to identify. It can be seen as a list of attributes that might be used to emphasise one's position in a couple. Debilitative power is harder to recognise, since it is often applied secretly, as Gatrell emphasises: 'in situations when the personal needs of one partner are suppressed by the other' (2007, p. 358). Gatrell claims that situational power is usually held by mothers, whereas debilitative power by fathers, yet I would argue that it depends to which right of choice one refers to.

Considering the right of choice to engage in satisfactory paid work, I argue that fathers have situational power, which is grounded in gender beliefs that a good father needs to provide for his family. Thus the question about men taking a break from paid work hardly ever appears in the context of becoming a parent. Yet at the same time, as I showed in Chap. 4, women's participation in the labour market is more often perceived in terms of bringing satisfaction and fulfilment. This might suggest that in a way a woman could more easily wield debilitative power and resign (at least temporarily) from paid work. If she resigns from paid work, the economic pressure is even greater on the father, and his choice is even more constrained. Of course, lack of paid work in a couple can lead to a relationship of dependency, which is characteristic of unemployed housewives. Thus this type of debilitative power is advantageous in the long term only when a woman has a good situation in the labour market and can easily find a job after some period of unemployment.

Concerning the three other rights of choice, women hold situational power, whereas men have debilitative power. A women's right to use parental leave is never questioned—it is grounded in gender beliefs and cultural norms about care. Consequently, women take more parental leave and have better arguments in front of their partners or husbands, as well as their employers and significant others. At the same time, fathers easily fall into the role of secondary caregiver. For many of them it is easier, especially when a child is small, not to be solely responsible for taking care of the child. Parental leave can be a very difficult period for many parents, so the right to choose if a parent wants to take it and for how long should be seen as an important right. As was argued in Chap. 3, care work is more satisfying when an individual is not forced to carry it out.

On the matter of the right to choose how care work is organised, especially after the period of paid parental leave, women also hold situational power, which is based on the fact that they spend more time with a child at the very beginning and so gain the necessary knowledge of how to take care of them. But at the same time, when there is a lack of support from the welfare state and parents need to fill the care gap resulting from the lack of places in care institutions, men are in a privileged position resulting from debilitative power, which allows them to concentrate on paid work whilst not taking into consideration, for example, a woman's need to return to paid work. Consequently, women are more often forced to take a break from paid work in connection to parenthood than men. Finally, concerning the right to choose the level of engagement in domestic work, it is clear that men's debilitative power not to engage in household duties lies in gender beliefs that they are an area of expertise for women, and as I demonstrated in Chap. 5, men use different types of excuses not to get engaged. At the same time, women wield situational power by maintaining the position of manager in everyday life.

It is hard to clearly state which type of power is more advantageous. Yet it is clear that men and women hold debilitative power in areas which are not traditionally associated with their gender. So women have debilitative power in the context of paid work, whereas men in the context of care and domestic work. This explains to some extent how gender inequalities prevail in contemporary times, regardless of the increasing participation of women in the labour market and the greater involvement of men in care and domestic duties. What is more, it also shows why couples are relapsing into gender inequality after becoming parents, even those couples who had an equalitarian approach beforehand (Reimann 2019). The normative models of motherhood and fatherhood are so deeply rooted in society that men and women can unconsciously seize the power rooted in them. Such power is grounded in the broader structures of gender inequalities, norms about care, the way the labour market functions, and how the family policy system is designed. All of these differently shape the opportunity structures available to men and women.

Apart from gender inequalities, my analysis also shows that economic inequalities are particularly important. In the case of each of these rights to choose, economic resources give more power and significantly broaden an individual's opportunity structures. Economic resources allow them to take a break from paid work or use unpaid leave, which provides greater opportunities in choosing how to organise care work—hire a baby-sitter or send a child to a nursery. Economic resources are also very important in of the area of domestic work, since they make it possible to outsource household chores to other people or invest in more effective household appliances. The current family policy system does not recognise these differences and does not provide different rights in connection to economic inequalities. Similarly, the situation of single parents is much more difficult than the situation of coupled parents, since single parents are often deprived of the support of a second person in fulfilling different parental obligations.

## 6.3 The Welfare State and Parenting Experiences

The welfare state plays an important role in designing the opportunity structures of parents. Its impact is especially evident in how care work and paid work are organised. My aim in this book has been to show how Polish parents experience parenthood and deal with its various obligations in the context of Polish family policy. I argue that such an approach is important not only from a sociological perspective, but also from the perspective of policy-makers. In designing family policy there is a need to look at the experiences of parents, who should be perceived as reflexive agents assessing their opportunity structures. Consequently, their experiences can indicate if the family system works and what should be improved or changed. In the context of my research, it is important to underline that the Polish family system in 2017 is characterised by an explicit familialism (Szelewa 2017), which means that it strengthens the family in caring for children (and other dependent family members) and does not provide many alternatives (Leitner 2003). My analysis clearly shows that parents with children under three face many difficulties in organising care after the end of parental leave. The Polish system has a care gap, which results from the incongruency of the parental leave system with institutional care for children. The support of the state is not sufficient, and many parents need to organise care using their own resources. Furthermore, as Mary Daly (2011) notes, familialistic systems treat family not in terms of individuals but as family members. The family as a whole is seen as the recipient of family policy instruments. Therefore, parental leave in the Polish system is not an individual entitlement of a mother or a father, but is a right of both parents that can be shared. Parents also have individual forms of leave—maternity leave for women, and paternity leave for men, yet they are not symmetrical. Women have a right to 20 weeks of maternity leave (from which 14 weeks are obligatory and 6 weeks can be transferred to the father), whereas men have a right to two weeks of untransferable paternity leave. Parental leave, even though it is the shared entitlement of a couple, is usually perceived as an extension of maternity leave, so consequently it is used by women (see Chap. 3). Such a system is explicitly genderising, since it perceives mothers as the main caregiver, whereas the role of a father is seen as a secondary caregiver or the mother's helper (Saxonberg 2013; Suwada 2017).

The issue of gender inequalities is hardly ever mentioned by Polish policy-makers nor do they provide any incentives to encourage fathers to be more engaged in taking care of their children. In familialistic states, men have greater choice of how much they want to be involved in family life, consequently their situation in the labour market is privileged compared to that of women. The aim of family policy in the European context is to support parents in the reconciliation of parenthood with paid work (Lewis 2006). At the same time, in recent decades we can observe the promotion of the adult worker model, in which high labour participation of all adults is expected (Daly 2011; Lewis and Giullari 2006). The Polish labour market is characterised by a high percentage of adults working full-time. According to Eurostat data[1] part-time employment is not as popular in Poland as in other European countries. All of the above points—the expectation that all adults work full-time, insufficient provision of institutional care for children under three, and strong gender roles in family life—make it especially difficult for women to reconcile paid work with parenthood. In a way the current system does not recognise gender inequalities yet at the same time it reinforces them. Similarly, it does not recognise the economic inequalities between different families. Although it is true that there are special cash benefits aimed at the poorest families, their value is usually very low, as is the income threshold criterion. Consequently, many families experiencing poverty do not receive any additional support. At the same time the most expensive programme of family policy in the twenty-first century, 'Family 500 +', was extended in 2019 to all children regardless of the financial situation of the family. In such a way, the opportunity structures of parents with different economic resources differ significantly. Those who can afford to pay for care in the free market are in a much more privileged position in comparison to those who cannot afford it. From an intersectional perspective, the only choice for low-skilled/low-income mothers to fill the care gap is to temporarily withdraw from the labour market, which is particularly difficult for them. In the long term such a withdrawal might lead to their greater marginalisation in the labour market and greater risk of poverty. The situation of single parents or parents of children with severe disabilities is even more problematic, and the reconciliation of paid work with parenthood is for many of them out of reach.

---

[1]Data available at: https://ec.europa.eu/eurostat/databrowser/view/tesem100/default/table?lang=en (accessed 21-09-2020).

The results of my research suggest that policy-makers in Poland should put more focus on economic and gender inequalities, and take these into account especially when designing the systems of parental leave and institutional care of children. There is also a need to look carefully at policies concerning the labour market and full-time employment. The narratives of Polish parents indicate that the possibility to work part-time would significantly help them in the organisation of care and domestic work. Yet part-time employment need not be connected with a significant reduction in salary. Reasonable and stable pay for work is a crucial issue for Polish parents, since having children requires economic resources. Salaries in Poland are at a very low level compared to some other European countries. Thus in designing family policy instruments it is crucial to include considerations on the labour market and the quality of work.

## 6.4 What Is Lacking in the Analysis?

In my analysis I have concentrated on the experience of parenthood in Polish society through the lens of three types work. This is obviously a limited perspective, therefore there is a need for further research that would provide more distance from the concept of a work/life balance. The issues that in my opinion would require greater focus are connected to the dimension of time. As I pointed out in Chap. 5 most parents complain about a lack of time—this results from multiple reasons, in particular from: full-time employment, demanding care work, and an increasing amount of domestic duties. Thus research on the leisure time of parents would add an interesting angle to research on parenting from the perspective of work. Anna Zachorowska-Mazurkiewicz (2016) claims that the difference between work and leisure is sometimes difficult to recognise, and that many people work for pleasure. This also applies to care work—whether time spent going for a walk with a child is leisure time or care time? Is it possible to distinguish these two aspects of parenthood? Certain domestic duties might also be perceived as giving pleasure. For example, there are people who like cooking. Yet does this mean that all cooking is similarly pleasant? Why are some activities associated with care/paid/domestic work seen as pleasurable while others are not? What is the difference between men and women in this regard? In my interviews some parents raised this issue, yet because it was not the main theme of the research, they did not elaborate on it. It would be necessary to design new research that would help to answer the above-mentioned questions.

In my research, I concentrated on economic and gender inequalities, yet it is clear that gender and economic dimensions are not the only dimensions that differentiate the situation of parents. In the research sample there were also single parents, as well as parents of children with disabilities. Even though my initial aim was to more systematically compare their situations with coupled parents, as well as parents of healthy children, during the analysis it became clear that it is not always possible to do so. Such a comparison is especially difficult in the case of parents with disabled children, whose situation is so different it is often incomparable. Their narratives about different types of work were differently constructed. The three types of work distinguished in this publication often overlap in their experiences. Consequently, their voice is often missing in the above analysis. Therefore, I have decided to analyse the situation of parents with children with disabilities separately in other publications.

In the preceding chapters I have tried to include the perspective of single parents. Yet it was not always possible. Today people raise children in different family configurations. The interviewed single parents also varied in their family situations. Some of them were totally alone from the very beginning because their partner did not participate in their children's life at all (for various reasons). Other single parents had raised children with their then partner prior to separation, when they henceforth raised them in alternating custody. Some single parents were in a new relationship, yet since the new partner did not participate in raising the child, they defined themselves as single parents. Consequently, it was impossible to include all of these perspectives in this book. Research on single parenthood would also require more careful sampling to include these multifarious perspectives.

In my analysis, I have usually referred to research conducted in Western European countries. I still lack enough studies published in English about other post-communist European countries. I argue here that the analysis of the experiences of Polish parents supplements the studies on parenting in Western Europe. I hope that my book will encourage other scholars from the peripheries of Europe to share their research and results with others.

Of course, as the sociology of families shows, there is a multitude of other topics associated with parenting that should be raised. Here, I indicated the most important ones that arise from my research. Parenting is a phenomenon that is constantly changing and is heavily dependent on social, cultural and institutional contexts. My book has attempted to describe the experiences of parenting in Polish society at the beginning of the twenty-first century. I hope that it fills some gaps in our current knowledge.

# References

Blofield, M., & Martinez Franzoni, J. (2015). Maternalism, co-responsibility, and social equity: A typology of work-family policies. *Social Politics: International Studies in Gender, State & Society, 22*(1), 38–59. https://doi.org/10.1093/sp/jxu015.

Bozionelos, N., & Hughes, J. (2007). Work-life balance as source of job dissatisfaction and withdrawal attitudes: An exploratory study on the views of male workers. *Personnel Review, 36*(1), 145–154. https://doi.org/10.1108/00483480710716768.

Caracciolo di Torella, E., & Masselot, A. (2010). *Reconciling work and family life in EU law and policy*. Palgrave Macmillan.

Daly, M. (2011). What adult worker model? A critical look at recent social policy reform in Europe from a gender and family perspective. *Social Politics: International Studies in Gender, State & Society, 18*(1), 1–23. https://doi.org/10.1093/sp/jxr002.

Doucet, A. (2004). 'It's almost like I have a job, but I don't get paid': Fathers at home reconfiguring work, care, and masculinity. *Fathering: A Journal of Theory, Research, and Practice about Men as Fathers, 2*(3), 277–303. https://doi.org/10.3149/fth.0203.277.

Dowd, N. E. (2000). *Redefining fatherhood*. New York University Press.

Drobnič, S. (2011). Introduction: Job quality and work-life balance. In S. Drobnič & A. M. Guillén (Eds.), *Work-life balance in Europe: The role of job quality*. Palgrave Macmillan.

Elliott, K. (2016). Caring masculinities theorizing an emerging concept. *Men and Masculinities, 19*(3), 240–259. https://doi.org/10.1177/1097184X15576203.

Gatrell, C. (2007). Whose child is it anyway? The negotiation of paternal entitlements within marriage. *The Sociological Review, 55*(2), 352–372. https://doi.org/10.1111/j.1467-954X.2007.00709.x.

Hanlon, N. (2012). *Masculinities, care and equality*. Palgrave Macmillan UK.

Hook, J. L. (2010). Gender inequality in the welfare state: Sex segregation in housework, 1965–2003. *American Journal of Sociology, 115*(5), 1480–1523.

Leitner, S. (2003). Varieties of familialism: The caring function of the family in comparative perspective. *European Societies, 5*(4), 353–375. https://doi.org/10.1080/1461669032000127642.

Lewis, J. (2006). Work/family reconciliation, equal opportunities and social policies: The interpretation of policy trajectories at the EU level and the meaning of gender equality. *Journal of European Public Policy, 13*(3), 420–437. https://doi.org/10.1080/13501760600560490.

Lewis, J., & Giullari, S. (2006). The adult-worker-model family and gender equality: Principles to enable the valuing and sharing of care. In S. Razavi & S. Hassim (Eds.), *Gender and social policy in a global context: Uncovering the gendered structure of 'the social'* (pp. 173–190). Palgrave Macmillan UK. https://doi.org/10.1057/9780230625280_8.

Nordenmark, M. (2002). Multiple social roles — A resource or a burden: Is it possible for men and women to combine paid work with family life in a satisfactory way? *Gender, Work & Organization, 9*(2), 125–145. https://doi.org/10.1111/1468-0432.00152.

Reimann, M. (2019). It is not something we consciously do: Polish couples struggles to maintain gender equality after the birth of their first child. In D. Grunow & M. Evertsson (Eds.), *New parents in Europe. Work-care practices, gender norms and family policies* (pp. 188–206). Edward Elgar Publishing.

Saxonberg, S. (2013). From defamilialization to degenderization: Toward a new welfare typology. *Social Policy & Administration, 47*(1), 26–49. https://doi.org/10.1111/j.1467-9515.2012.00836.x.

Scambor, E., Bergmann, N., Wojnicka, K., Belghiti-Mahut, S., Hearn, J., Holter, Ø. G., et al. (2014). Men and gender equality: European insights. *Men and Masculinities, 17*(5), 552–577. https://doi.org/10.1177/1097184X14558239.

Smart, C., & Neale, B. (1998). *Family fragments?* Polity Press.

Sullivan, O. (2013). What do we learn about gender by analyzing housework separately from child care? Some considerations from time-use evidence. *Journal of Family Theory & Review, 5*(2), 72–84. https://doi.org/10.1111/jftr.12007.

Suwada, K. (2015). Naturalisation of the difference. The experience of fatherhood in Sweden and Poland. *Studia Humanistyczne AGH, 2*(16), 141–155. https://doi.org/10.7494/human.2015.14.2.141.

Suwada, K. (2017). *Men, fathering and the gender trap. Sweden and Poland compared*. Palgrave Macmillan.

Szelewa, D. (2017). From implicit to explicit familialism: Post-1989 family policy reforms in Poland. In *Gender and family in European economic policy* (pp. 129–151). Cham: Palgrave Macmillan.

Wall, G., & Arnold, S. (2007). How involved is involved fathering? An exploration of the contemporary culture of fatherhood. *Gender & Society, 21*(4), 508–527. https://doi.org/10.1177/0891243207304973.

Zachorowska-Mazurkiewicz, A. (2016). *Praca kobiet w teorii ekonomii: Perspektywa ekonomii głównego nurtu i ekonomii feministycznej.* Wydawnictwo Uniwersytetu Jagiellońskiego.

**Open Access** This chapter is licensed under the terms of the Creative Commons Attribution 4.0 International License (http://creativecommons.org/licenses/by/4.0/), which permits use, sharing, adaptation, distribution and reproduction in any medium or format, as long as you give appropriate credit to the original author(s) and the source, provide a link to the Creative Commons license and indicate if changes were made.

The images or other third party material in this chapter are included in the chapter's Creative Commons license, unless indicated otherwise in a credit line to the material. If material is not included in the chapter's Creative Commons license and your intended use is not permitted by statutory regulation or exceeds the permitted use, you will need to obtain permission directly from the copyright holder.

The manufacturer's authorised representative in the EU is Springer Nature Customer Service Centre GmbH, Europaplatz 3, 69115 Heidelberg, Germany. If you have any concerns regarding our products, please contact ProductSafety@springernature.com

Printed and bound by CPI Group (UK) Ltd, Croydon, CR0 4YY

25/03/2026

02078227-0001